Programming Fundamentals
in JavaScript

Published by Maia L.L.C.
Idaho, U.S.A.

ISBN 978-0-9962463-3-0

The author and publisher of this book have used their best efforts in preparing this book, and the information contained in this book is believed to be reliable. These efforts include the development, research, and testing of the theories and computer programs in this book to determine their correctness. However, because of the possibility of human or mechanical error, the author and publisher make no warranty of any kind, expressed or implied, with regard to these programs or the documentation or information contained in this book. The author and publisher shall not be liable in any event for incidental or consequential damages in connection with or arising out of the furnishing, performance, or use of these programs.

Contents

Preface   ix
    How to Use This Book   ix
    Conventions   ix
    Acknowledgments   x
    Review This Book   x

Chapter 1 . Computer Hardware   1
    Chapter Outcome   1
    Semiconductors   1
    Parts of a Computer   2
    Data Sizes   4
    Clock Speeds   5
    Classes of Computers   5
    Categories of Software   6
    Character Data   6
    Execution Example   7
    Review Questions   7

Chapter 2 . Algorithms and Computer Programs   9
    Chapter Outcomes   9
    Defining Table   9
    Algorithms   10
    Computer Programs   11
    Computer Operations   12
    Control Structures   12
    Chapter Summary   13
    Review Questions   13

Chapter 3 . HTML Basics   15
    Chapter Outcomes   15
    Starting with HTML   15
    Document Type Declaration   15
    Comments   15
    HTML Elements   16
    Case Insensitive   18
    Well Formed HTML   18
    Required Elements   18
    Example HTML Document   19
    Example HTML Document with a Form   20
    Common Mistakes   22
    Chapter Summary   23
    Review Questions   23
    Assignments   24

Chapter 4 . JavaScript Basics   25

Chapter Outcomes   25
Starting with JavaScript   25
Running a Program   26
Comments   26
Statements   27
Case Sensitive   27
Declaring Variables   27
String Concatenation   27
Popup Windows   28
Text Fields and Divisions   29
Reserved Words   31
Fixing a Program that Doesn't Work 32
Common Mistakes   32
Chapter Summary   32
Review Questions   33
Programming Assignments   34

Chapter 5 . Variables and Arithmetic   35

Chapter Outcomes   35
Declaring a Variable   35
Variable Types   36
Assigning to a Variable   36
Desk Checks   37
Swapping Values   38
Arithmetic Expressions   39
Arithmetic Operators   39
Operator Precedence   40
Celsius to Fahrenheit   40
Fahrenheit to Celsius   42
Assignment Operators   43
Increment and Decrement Operators   44
Operator Precedence Revisited   46
Math Object   47
Volume of a Cylinder   48
Round to Decimal Places   50
Common Mistakes   52
Chapter Summary   53
Review Questions   53
Programming Assignments   55

Chapter 6 . Selection 59

Chapter Outcomes 59
Relational Operators 59
if … 60
if … else … 61
if … else if … else … 63
Power of else 64
switch 66
Even Integers 67
Odd Integers 68
Quadratic Formula 69
Nested If Statements 71
Common Mistakes 76
Chapter Summary 77
Review Questions 77
Programming Assignments 78

Chapter 7 . Logic 81

Chapter Outcomes 81
Logical Operators 81
Choosing a Group 82
Disneyland Autopia 85
Exclusive Or 87
Logical Equivalences 88
Using De Morgan's Law 90
Advanced Word Search 91
Truth Tables 92
Common Mistakes 97
Chapter Summary 98
Review Questions 98
Programming Assignments 100

Chapter 8 . Repetition 103

Chapter Outcomes 103
Pre-test and Post-test Loops 103
Counting and Sentinel Controlled Loops 104
Repetition Control Structures 104
while 104
for 105
For Each Loop 106
do while 106
Simple Counting Loop 107
Zero-Based Counting Loop 108
Skipping Loop 108
Infinite Loop 109
Compound Interest 110
break 111
Prime Numbers 112

Repetitive Strings   115
Common Mistakes   116
Chapter Summary   117
Review Questions   117
Programming Assignments   121

Chapter 9 . Functions   123

Chapter Outcomes   123
Writing a Function   123
Calling a Function   125
Variable Scope   127
Advantages of Functions   128
Pseudo Random Integer   128
Code Reuse   129
Area of a Triangle   131
Surface Area of a Pyramid   132
How Long to Invest   134
Greatest Common Divisor   135
Common Mistakes   137
Chapter Summary   138
Review Questions   138
Programming Assignments   139

Chapter 10 . Arrays   147

Chapter Outcomes   147
Declaring an Array   147
Creating an Array   148
Array Length   149
Accessing an Element   149
Filling an Array   150
Filling an Array with a Ramp   151
Reversing an Array   153
Summing the Values in an Array   153
Finding a Value (Linear Search)   154
Parallel Arrays   154
Finding a Range   156
Finding a Value (Binary Search)   160
Array Methods   162
Sorting an Array   163
Sorting Numbers   166
Common Mistakes   168
Chapter Summary   169
Review Questions   170
Programming Assignments   170

Chapter 11 . Objects   177

Chapter Outcomes   177
Objects and Classes   177
Unified Modeling Language   178
Relationships   178
Multiplicities   179
JavaScript Built-in Objects   182
Declaring an Object   182
Creating an Object   182
Accessing an Attribute   183
Calling a Method   184
Dictionaries   184
Local Storage   185
Document Object Model   187
Chapter Summary   189
Review Questions   190
Programming Assignments   191

Chapter 12 . Strings   193

Chapter Outcomes   193
Creating a String   193
String Concatenation   193
Escape Sequences   194
String Length   195
Accessing a Character   195
Reversing a String   196
Comparing Strings   196
String Methods   197
Extracting a Substring   198
Counting Characters   198
Transposing Chords   199
Chapter Summary   202
Review Questions   202
Programming Assignments   203

Appendix A. Operator Precedence   205

Associativity   205
Precedence   206

Appendix B. Robust Code   207

Appendix C. Answers to Selected Desk Checks 209

Chapter 5. Variables and Arithmetic   209
Chapter 6. Selection   209
Chapter 7. Logic   210
Chapter 8. Repetition   210
Chapter 9. Functions   212
Chapter 10. Arrays   213
Chapter 12. Strings   215

Appendix D. Answers to Selected Review Questions
217

Chapter 1. Computer Hardware   217
Chapter 2. Algorithms and Computer Programs   218
Chapter 3. HTML Basics   218
Chapter 4. JavaScript Basics   219
Chapter 5. Variables and Arithmetic   219
Chapter 6. Selection   221
Chapter 7. Logic   222
Chapter 8. Repetition   223
Chapter 9. Functions   225
Chapter 10. Arrays   225
Chapter 11. Objects   226
Chapter 12. Strings   226

Index   227

Preface

Learning to program a computer is a frustrating task for many students. In my teaching experience, I have found that much of this frustration comes because students are not shown enough programming examples. All of us learn by watching others, so why should learning to program a computer be any different? I wrote this book with minimal text but filled with computer programming examples and many hands on exercises to help beginning students learn computer programming more efficiently and thoroughly and with less frustration.

How to Use This Book

You can use this book as a tutorial or a reference. When using it as a tutorial, you will find it helpful to step through the example code line by line as if you were a computer. Doing this is sometimes called a **desk check** because you are checking the code on paper or "at your desk" instead of running it on a computer. To aid you in desk checking the example code, I have provided desk check locations throughout the book. Each desk check location includes a list of all the variables found in the corresponding example code and values for the input variables. To perform a desk check, step through the code as if you were the computer and change the value of each variable just as the computer would.

Conventions

Within the text of this book, the following fonts and font styles are used.

- **Bolded text** is used to highlight an important term.
- *Italicized text* emphasizes certain words that might be missed by casual reading.
- <u>Underlined text</u> indicates a hyperlink to a website.
- `Fixed width font` is used to show computer code.
- Menu font shows the words that appear in a computer menu or on a computer button.

Chapters 5–12 include JavaScript code templates that use these fonts and symbols.

- `Fixed width font` is used for JavaScript keywords that you must type exactly as they are shown in the template.
- *Italicized text* is used for words that you should replace when you write code.
- Any part of a template that is written in gray text is optional.

For example within the following template, var is a JavaScript keyword, *name*, *name2*, and *name3* should be replaced by names that you choose, and *name2* and *name3* are optional.

```
var name, name2, name3…;
```

Several locations in this book use brackets and parentheses to specify an interval or range of numbers, like this [0, 25). A bracket means that end of the interval is inclusive, or in other words includes the listed number. A parenthesis means that end of the interval is exclusive, or in other words excludes the listed number. For example, in this interval: [0, 25), 0 is included, but 25 is excluded.

To aid in your learning, this book contains different types of learning tools such as

- example code with tables to desk check that code
- review questions
- programming assignments

Locations within this book where you should write or do an exercise are marked in the

margin with a pencil icon like this

Acknowledgments

I am grateful to Michael McLaughlin for our many discussions on pedagogy and student learning. I thank my wife for her support and proofreading of this book. I am also grateful to my students who have used this book and given me valuable suggestions, such as Adam Martin, one of my teaching assistants, who gave me valuable suggestions about the chapter on functions.

The quick response (QR) codes in this book were provided by kaywa at qrcode.kaywa.com The ISBN barcode was provided by Terry Burton at www.terryburton.co.uk/barcodewriter/generator

Review This Book

Please rate this book or write a review at www.amazon.com/dp/B0727XJR94. Your comments and suggestions help the author and publisher produce better books.

Chapter 1. Computer Hardware

Chapter Outcome

By the end of this chapter, you will have a basic understanding of computer hardware so that you can begin to program computers.

Semiconductors

Many of the parts of a computer, including the CPU and main memory, are composed of millions or billions of microscopic semiconductors that are etched in silicon. The word semiconductor means these microscopic parts partially conduct or sometimes conduct electricity. There are many different types of semiconductors, and each type fulfills a specific purpose. Below is a list of common semiconductors and their purpose.

1. Capacitor – a semiconductor that temporarily stores electricity.

2. Diode – a semiconductor that allows electricity to flow in only one direction.

3. LED – acronym for light emitting diode; a diode that emits light when electricity is flowing through it.

4. Resistor – a semiconductor that resists the flow of electricity. A resistor is often used to protect other parts of a computer from surges in electricity.

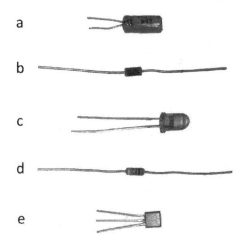

Figure 1-1: Photographs of common semiconductors: a) capacitor, b) diode, c) light emitting diode, d) resistor, and e) transistor.

5. Transistor – a semiconductor with two inputs and one output called the drain. A small current on the center wire of the transistor controls a larger current that flows on the two outer wires. A transistor can be used as an amplifier or an automated switch with the small electric current input controlling the larger input and output current.

6. Integrated circuit – a circuit composed of many (possibly billions) semiconductors etched on a small piece of silicon; sometimes called a computer chip.

Parts of a Computer

A modern computer is an electronic machine that is composed of two major parts: hardware and software. Computer hardware is the physical parts of a computer, such as the keyboard, mouse, CPU, hard drive, memory, monitor, and printer. An easy mnemonic to help you remember that hardware is the physical parts of a computer is that the physical parts are hard. If someone threw a piece of computer hardware at you, and it hit you, it would hurt. Of course, each part of a computer has its own specific purpose. Here is a list of common computer hardware parts.

7. Power supply – an electric circuit that converts the electricity coming from an outlet in the wall, usually 115 volts, 60-Hertz alternating current (AC), into electricity that a computer can use, such as 3.3 volts direct current (DC).

8. Keyboard – an input device that allows a user to enter data into a computer by pressing keys.

9. Motherboard – the main circuit board to which the other parts of a computer are attached. Figure 1-2 shows a computer motherboard without a CPU, main memory, or other devices attached to it.

Figure 1-2: A computer motherboard.

10. Bus – the wires and integrated circuits that transfer data across the motherboard from one component to another.

11. BIOS – acronym for basic input and output system; usually flash memory installed on the motherboard that contains instructions the CPU executes when a computer is started.

12. CPU – acronym for central processing unit; a relatively large and expensive integrated circuit where most calculations are done within a computer.

13. Cache – a small amount of fast memory that temporarily stores data and instructions and is often located on the CPU. The cache contains a partial copy of the contents of main memory so that when the CPU needs data for a calculation, the CPU can get the data from the cache and does not have to wait for the data to come over a bus from main memory. Cache memory is **volatile** which means that when a computer is turned off or the electricity is removed, the contents of cache are lost.

Figure 1-3: The top and bottom of an Intel Core i7 processor. Picture is courtesy of Intel.

14. Main memory – integrated circuits that temporarily store data and instructions for the CPU; sometimes called random access memory (RAM). Main memory is volatile which means that when a computer is turned off, the contents of main memory are lost.

Figure 1-4: Four gigabytes of DDR random access memory. Photo is courtesy of newegg.com.

15. Hard drive – stores data semi-permanently usually on a spinning platter where microscopic spots have been magnetized to store data. A hard drive is **non-volatile** which means that when a computer is turned off, the contents of a hard drive are preserved. Figure 1-5 shows a hard drive with its cover removed to expose the platter and the head that moves above the platter and magnetizes microscopic spots on the platter.

Figure 1-5: A computer hard drive with its cover removed exposing the platter and the head that moves above the platter. Photo is courtesy of Evan-Amos at en.wikipedia.org.

16. CD or DVD drive – reads and writes data semi-permanently to a disc using a laser. Compact discs (CD's) and digital versatile disks (DVD's) are non-volatile.

17. Jump, thumb, or flash drive – semi-permanent memory that can be read, written, and erased electrically. Jump drive, thumb drive, and flash drive are different names for the same type of memory device which stores data in flash memory. A solid state hard drive does not store data on a platter like a regular hard drive but instead stores data in flash memory. Flash memory is non-volatile.

18. Monitor – an output device that displays messages, images, etc. for a user to see.

Data Sizes

Each of the following terms is a measure of the amount of data that a computer can store or process.

19. bit – an abbreviation for binary digit. A binary digit is a column in a binary number where either 0 or 1 can appear

20. nibble – four bits joined together to form a binary number. The name nibble is an inside computing joke because a nibble is half of a byte.

21. byte – eight bits joined together to form a binary number.

22. kilobyte – a true kilobyte is 1024 (2^{10}) bytes and not just 1000 bytes.

23. megabyte – a true megabyte is 1,048,576 (2^{20}) bytes and not just 1,000,000 bytes.

24. gigabyte – 2^{30} bytes

25. terabyte – 2^{40} bytes

26. petabyte – 2^{50} bytes

27. exabyte – 2^{60} bytes

Clock Speeds

The clock within a CPU is a small electrical circuit that repeatedly produces an electric signal that pulses, meaning its voltage rises and falls similar to Figure 1-6. This electric signal pulses many times a second, and a single core on a CPU is designed to complete one instruction at the end of each pulse. Clock speed is measured in hertz. A single hertz is one cycle per second. A cycle is from any point in the pulse to where the pulse repeats. In other words, a single cycle starts immediately after the electric voltage falls, includes the voltage rising, and ends when the voltage falls again. Here are the terms used to measure clock speeds:

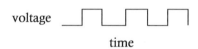

voltage

time

Figure 1-6: A graph of a pulsing electric signal showing three pulses or cycles.

28. hertz – a unit of frequency equal to one cycle per second

29. megahertz – one million cycles per second

30. gigahertz – one billion cycles per second.

Many modern computers have clock speeds of 2.5 gigahertz or higher which means a single core on a CPU is designed to complete 2.5 billion instructions per second. Many CPU's have multiple cores. Each core performs calculations independently of the other cores. A quad core CPU with a clock speed of 2.5 gigahertz is designed to complete 10 billion (4 * 2.5 gigahertz) instructions per second. This is very fast.

Classes of Computers

Computers can be classified according to their size and primary purpose. Here are some common computer classes.

31. micro or personal computer – a computer designed to be used by only one person at a time, such as a smart phone, tablet computer, laptop computer, or desktop computer.

32. workstation – a powerful computer designed to be used by one person at a time and used to perform engineering, scientific, and medical tasks such as designing airplane parts or modeling biological processes.

33. mainframe – a very powerful computer designed to be used by many people at the same time to perform business or scientific tasks.

Categories of Software

Computer hardware is really just a bunch of metal that electricity can flow through in well-defined paths. Computer hardware will not do anything without some instructions. The instructions are written by a computer programmer and are called software. Computer software is simply a list of instructions that the computer hardware executes. Computer software can be classified according to its purpose.

34. Application – computer software that someone uses to accomplish a specific task, such as write a letter, balance an account, watch a movie, or play a game. Examples of applications include Microsoft Word and Excel, Google Chrome, and iTunes.

35. Operating system – computer software that manages the hardware and isolates the applications from the hardware so that the applications do not have to interact directly with the hardware. Examples of computer operating systems include Microsoft Windows, Mac OS X, VMS, Linux, HP-UX, and Solaris.

Character Data

Everything in a computer's memory is stored as a number or set of numbers. Everything. Pictures, songs, text, instructions, everything. Each text symbol is stored in the computer's memory as a number.

36. ASCII – an acronym for American Standard Code for Information Interchange; a coding system (essentially a table) with 128 rows that assigns a number to each English letter and common punctuation symbol. See asciitable.com

37. Unicode – a very large coding system that includes ASCII and assigns a number to symbols from many languages, such as English, Portuguese, Greek, Hebrew, Arabic, and Tagalog. See unicode.org

Execution Example

To help you understand how the parts of a computer work together, consider what happens when a user double clicks on a Microsoft Word document file (a file with a filename suffix of .docx).

1. The operating system commands the hard drive to copy the Microsoft Word Application (MS Word) into main memory.
2. The hard drive copies MS Word over a bus into main memory.
3. After MS Word is in main memory, the operating system executes MS Word and sends a command to MS Word telling it to open the document that the user double clicked.
4. MS Word requests the operating system to read the document from the hard drive and to place it in main memory.
5. The operating system commands the hard drive to copy the document file into main memory.
6. The hard drive copies the document file over a bus into main memory.
7. For each character that is in the document
    a. MS Word reads the character's Unicode number from main memory and requests the operating system to draw that character in a window.
    b. The operating system finds the Unicode number and its corresponding symbol in a table and draws the symbol.

Review Questions

1. Which of the following is primarily used to store data? (Mark all that apply.)
    a. power supply
    b. keyboard
    c. motherboard
    d. bus
    e. CPU
    f. cache
    g. main memory
    h. hard drive
    i. digital versatile disc (DVD)
    j. thumb drive or jump drive
    k. monitor

2. Match each of the following types of computer memory with the physical quantity that each manipulates to store data.
    a. cache
    b. main memory
    c. flash memory
    d. hard drive
    e. DVD drive

    i. light
    ii. magnetization
    iii. electric charge

3. Computer memory that is volatile must have electricity in order to store data. When electricity is turned off, volatile memory loses its data. Non-volatile memory stores data after electricity is turned off. Which of the following computer memory devices are volatile? (Mark all that apply.)
   a. cache
   b. main memory
   c. flash memory
   d. hard drive
   e. DVD

4. Match each term to its corresponding size in bytes.
   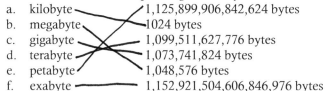
   a. kilobyte   1,125,899,906,842,624 bytes
   b. megabyte   1024 bytes
   c. gigabyte   1,099,511,627,776 bytes
   d. terabyte   1,073,741,824 bytes
   e. petabyte   1,048,576 bytes
   f. exabyte   1,152,921,504,606,846,976 bytes

5. Assume the average movie uses 3 gigabytes of space on a hard drive. Which of these is the smallest size that can store 200 average size movies?
   a. 500 megabytes
   b. 500 gigabytes
   c. 1 terabyte
   d. 1 petabyte

6. Consider a quad core CPU with a clock speed of 2.8 gigahertz. In theory, how many instructions per second is it able to complete?
   a. 2.8 million
   b. 2.8 billion
   c. 11.2 billion
   d. 20 billion

7. If you wanted to type a letter in Hebrew, which character coding system would your computer need to use to store your letter?
   a. ASCII
   b. Unicode

8. Which character coding system includes English letters? (Mark all that apply.)
   a. ASCII
   b. Unicode

Chapter 2. Algorithms and Computer Programs

Chapter Outcomes

By the end of this chapter, you will:

- Read a description of a problem and write a defining table to help you better understand the problem.
- Develop an algorithm for a common task.
- Understand the basic operations that a computer can perform.
- Learn the three basic control structures: sequence, selection, and repetition, and learn what they cause a computer to do.

Defining Table

An **algorithm** is simply a list of steps to perform some task. A large computer program contains many algorithms. Before creating an algorithm to solve a problem, you must be sure that you understand the problem. If you don't, you will probably create an algorithm that solves the wrong problem. A **defining table** is a useful tool to help you better understand a problem before you develop an algorithm to solve it. A defining table has three sections: input, processing, and output. To create a defining table, simply draw a table with the three sections. Then as you read and re-read the problem, put the parts of the problem into their correct section in the table.

Example 1

You work for a large construction company. Your boss has asked you to write a computer program that will read a list of window openings for a building, and compute and output the total cost of all the windows. The window openings are entered in inches with the width first and the height second. The cost of a window is computed by multiplying the area of the window in square feet by $35.

Defining Table

Input	Processing	Output
A list of window openings For each window • width in inches • height in inches	For each window • compute area in sq. ft. • multiply area by $35 • add cost of this window to the total cost	total cost of all windows

Example 2

You have been asked to write a program that will read from the keyboard the radius of a circle and will output to the monitor the diameter, circumference, and area of the circle.

Defining Table

Input	Processing	Output
radius	Compute Diameter by: $d = 2r$ Compute circumfrence : $C = 2\pi r$ compute area : $a = \pi r^2$	diameter circumference area

Algorithms

An **algorithm** is simply a list of steps to perform some task. A recipe is an example of an algorithm because the recipe lists the steps necessary for preparing some food. Here is a recipe from allrecipes.com for making chocolate chip cookies. Notice that the directions are what make a recipe similar to an algorithm.

Ingredients

- 1 cup butter, softened
- 1 cup white sugar
- 1 cup packed brown sugar
- 2 eggs
- 2 teaspoons vanilla extract
- 3 cups all-purpose flour
- 1 teaspoon baking soda
- 2 teaspoons hot water
- 1/2 teaspoon salt
- 2 cups semisweet chocolate chips
- 1 cup chopped walnuts

Directions

1. Preheat oven to 350 degrees F (175 degrees C).
2. Cream together the butter, white sugar, and brown sugar until smooth.
3. Beat in the eggs one at a time.
4. Stir in the vanilla.
5. Dissolve baking soda in hot water. Add to batter along with salt.
6. Stir in flour, chocolate chips, and nuts.
7. Drop by large spoonfuls onto ungreased pans.
8. Bake for about 10 minutes in the preheated oven, or until edges are nicely browned.

Programming Fundamentals in JavaScript

Example 3

Here is a small algorithm for computing the average test score from a list of test scores. Notice that it is nothing more than the step-by-step process for performing the calculation. A large computer program contains many algorithms.

1. Set *sum* to 0
2. Get the number of students
3. For each student
    a. Get the student's test score
    b. Add the student's score to the *sum*
4. Divide the *sum* by the number of students

Example 4

Write an algorithm to brush your teeth.

1. Get toothbrush + toothpaste - one in each hand
2. Squeeze toothpaste on to toothbrush bristles - a pea sized amount.
3. Put toothbrush in mouth
4. With scrubbing motion, push bristles back + forth on teeth, front + backs
5. Spit excess saliva when needed

Within the algorithm that you wrote, is the order of the steps important? Are there any steps that the order does not matter?

Computer Programs

A computer program is composed of data and instructions. The computer stores the data temporarily in its main memory. It also stores data more permanently in files on a hard drive, flash memory, or digital versatile disk (DVD). The instructions in a computer program are like the steps in an algorithm. In a programming language like JavaScript, the instructions are called statements. A single **statement** is equivalent to a single step in an algorithm or a single sentence in a paragraph. The statements tell the computer what to do with the data.

Computer Operations

A computer has seven basic operations that it can perform, all of which we can use when writing algorithms in a computer program. A computer can do the following:

1. Receive data (input)
    Input devices: keyboard, mouse, microphone, touch screen, temperature sensor, hard drive, flash drive, etc.

2. Write out data (output)
    Output devices: monitor, printer, speakers, lights, hard drive, flash drive, etc.

3. Assign a value to a variable or memory location

4. Perform arithmetic
    Operators: – (negation), * (multiplication), / (division), % (modulus), + (addition), – (subtraction)

5. Compare two values
    Relational operators: < (less than), <= (less than or equal), > (greater than), >= (greater than or equal), == (equal), != (not equal)

6. Repeat a group of actions

7. Call a function and return from that function

You will study and use each of these basic computer operations in later chapters of this text.

Control Structures

There are five different categories of **control structures** that you can use to control the order in which a computer executes the statements in your program. They are called control structures because they control the *order in which the computer executes statements* also called the **flow of execution**.

1. **sequence** – causes the computer to execute statements in the order they are written in a program, from top to bottom. This is the default control structure.

2. **selection** – causes the computer to select one group of statements to execute and another group or groups to skip. This is how a computer appears to make decisions.

3. **repetition** – causes the computer to repeat a group of statements.

4. **function call** and **return** – causes the computer to execute the statements in another function and return a result from the other function to the call point.

5. **try**, **catch**, and **throw** – are used to indicate an error occurred and to handle errors.

You will study, learn, and use the first four of these control structures in later chapters of this book. Sequence is the default control structure and is covered in chapters 4 – 12. Selection is taught in chapters 6 and 7. Repetition is taught in chapter 8 and again in chapter 10, and function call is taught in chapter 9.

Chapter Summary

- An algorithm is simply a list of steps to accomplish a task.
- Sometimes the order in which the steps are performed is very important.
- A defining table is a simple tool to help a programmer understand a problem before developing an algorithm to solve the problem. A defining table has three sections: input, processing, and output.
- A computer is capable of performing only a few basic operations:
    - receive input
    - display output
    - store data
    - perform arithmetic
    - compare values
    - repeat operations
    - call a function
- All high level tasks that a computer can do, such as edit photographs, play music, and search data are simply combinations of the basic operations.
- A computer program contains both data and instructions. In JavaScript, the instructions are called statements.
- The three basic control structures that a programmer uses to control the order in which a computer executes statements are sequence, selection, and repetition.

Review Questions

1. Your company needs a program to compute the amount to charge customers for mowing their lawns for an entire season. An employee will type in the total area of the customer's lawn in square feet. Your company charges 10 cents per square foot to mow a lawn one time and will mow each lawn once a week for 15 weeks. Write a defining table for this problem.

2. You have been asked to write a computer program that will output an employee's after tax pay. Your program will read from the keyboard the number of regular hours and overtime hours that the employee worked and the employee's regular hourly wage. The employee is paid a bonus of 1.5 times regular pay for each overtime hour worked. Tax is 15% of the employee's gross pay. Write a defining table for this problem.

3. Which of the following are control structures? (Mark all that apply.)
    a. input
    b. computation
    c. sequence
    d. selection
    e. repetition
    f. try, catch, and throw
    g. storage

Chapter 3. HTML Basics

Hypertext markup language (HTML) is a computer language that is used to write documents for the world wide web of information on the internet. There are several different versions of the HTML standard, with the most recent being XHTML 1.1 and HTML 5. This chapter will help you learn enough HTML 5 so that you can begin writing JavaScript code in your HTML documents.

Chapter Outcomes

By the end of this chapter, you will be able to:

- Read and write simple HTML 5 documents.
- Use the online W3C Markup Validation Service to validate that an HTML 5 document is well formed.
- Fix an HTML 5 document that does not validate.
- Use comments to add internal explanations to an HTML document.

Starting with HTML

To start writing HTML documents you must have a decent text editor, such as
VS Code (https://code.visualstudio.com),
Brackets (http://brackets.io), or
Sublime (http://www.sublimetext.com),
and a web browser, such as Google Chrome (https://www.google.com/chrome), installed on your computer. When you use your text editor to write an HTML document and then save the document, you must save the document with a suffix of `.html`

Document Type Declaration

All HTML 5 documents must begin with a document type declaration like this: `<!DOCTYPE HTML>`. It doesn't matter whether you write this declaration in upper or lower case or a mix of the two. This declaration tells the computer that what follows is an HTML 5 document. If you forget to put it at the top of an HTML document, your browser may recognize the document as an older version of HTML, and your browser may draw the document incorrectly.

Comments

A **comment** in an HTML document is a note or documentation that a web designer writes for himself or other designers who will look at the HTML code. The computer ignores comments. A comment in HTML begins with the symbols less than, exclamation mark, and two dashes, like this: `<!--` and ends with the symbols two dashes and greater than, like this: `-->`. *Way to take notes*

HTML Elements

An HTML **document** is composed of elements. An element is simply a part of an HTML document. Figure 3-1 shows an HTML element and all of its parts. Notice that an HTML **element** is composed of an opening tag, optional text, and a closing tag. A single **tag** begins with the less than symbol (<) and ends with the greater than symbol (>). For example `<div class="note" id="high">` or `</div>`. An opening tag contains a tag name and optionally some attributes. Each **attribute** is composed of a name and a value separated by an equal sign (=), such as `id="high"`. A closing tag has the same name as the opening tag, but the name is preceded by a slash character (/).

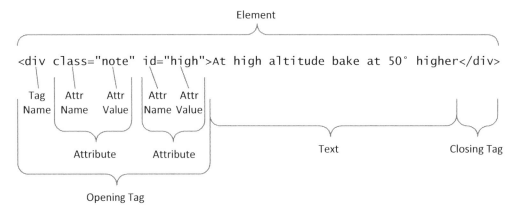

Figure 3-1: An HTML element and its parts. An element is composed of an opening tag, optional text, and a closing tag. An opening tag is composed of a tag name and optional attributes. An attribute is composed of a name and a value.

Sometimes the opening and closing tags are combined into one tag, such as:

`<input type="text" id="futureValue" size="5" />`

Notice the slash character (/), which is normally in the closing tag, is at the end of the `input` tag above. The slash character appears at the end of this `input` tag because this tag is both an opening and closing tag combined together.

Hypertext Markup Language (HTML) is really just a list of tags that most web browsers understand. The following table lists most of the HTML tags that we will use in this class. A good reference that describes these tags in more detail is at w3schools.com.

Opening and Closing Tags	Purpose
`<!DOCTYPE HTML>`	The document type declaration that must appear at the top of all HTML 5 documents. Technically, this declaration is not a tag, so it has no closing tag.
`<!-- a comment here -->`	A comment or notes seen only by the developers and not the users of a page. A comment is not a true tag, so it has no closing tag.
`<html lang="en-us">` `</html>`	Begins and ends an HTML document. These are the first and last tags of an HTML document.
`<head>` `</head>`	Marks the start and end of the HTML document head. Every HTML document must have one head. The head contains information such as the title and author of the document and most JavaScript code.
`<meta>`	Provides information about a document, such as the author, descriptions, keywords, and the character encoding. (No closing tag.)
`<title>` `</title>`	Marks the title of a document. This tag should appear in the document head.
`<script>` `</script>`	Marks the start and end of JavaScript code. You can place a <script> tag in the head or body of an HTML document, but they are normally placed in the head.
`<body>` `</body>`	Marks the start and end of the document body. Every HTML document must have one body. The body contains the main information of a document that the user will see.
`<h1>` `</h1>`	Marks the start and end of a level 1 heading. There are six different heading tags numbered from <h1> to <h6> with <h1> being the largest and <h6> being the smallest style of heading.
`<div>` `</div>`	Marks the start and end of a division within an HTML document. The concept of division in HTML is very general and is simply a large, medium, or small section of a document.
`<canvas>` `</canvas>`	Makes an area where a JavaScript program can draw shapes.
`<p>` `</p>`	Marks the limits of a paragraph.
`<b>` `</b>`	Marks the start and end of bold text. _Inline_
`<i>` `</i>`	Marks the start and end of italicized text. _Inline_

HTML Tags

Opening and Closing Tags	Purpose
` `	Forces the browser to insert a line break. (No closing tag.)
`<input type="text">`	Makes a text field (single row) where a user can enter data. (No closing tag.)
`<textarea>` `</textarea>`	Makes a text area (multiple rows) where a user can enter data.
`<button type="button">` `</button>`	Makes a button that a user can click.

Case Insensitive

HTML 5 is not case sensitive. This means that `<HTML>` and `<html>` and `<HtMl>` have the same meaning in HTML 5. However, the standard convention is to use all lower case for tags and attributes except for the DOCTYPE declaration, which is all uppercase. Most developers use lower case letters for at least two reasons:

1. Lower case letters are easier to read because they vary in size more than upper case letters.
2. If an HTML 5 document is ever converted to XHTML, which requires lower case tags and attributes, the conversion will be easier.

Well Formed HTML

An HTML document should be well formed which means:

1. The document contains only the standard tags and attributes.
2. Most opening tags have a matching closing tag. The opening tags that don't require a closing tag are called **void tags** and include `<meta>` `<br>` and `<input>`.
3. Nested tags are ended before their enclosing tags are ended, for example:

```
<body>
<p>Oregano is an important <i>culinary</i> herb. It is used in Greek and
Italian dishes especially tomato based sauces, fried vegetables, and
grilled meats.</p>
</body>
```

You can check an HTML document to ensure that it is well formed by uploading it to the online validator at validator.w3.org

Required Elements

Every HTML 5 document must start with a `<!DOCTYPE>` declaration and an opening `<html>` tag. Every HTML 5 document must have a head section and a body section, and the head section should have a `<title>` tag and a `<meta>` tag that states the document's character

Programming Fundamentals in JavaScript

encoding. In other words, the skeleton of every HTML 5 document should look similar to this:

```
<!DOCTYPE HTML>
<html lang="en-us">
<head>
<meta charset="utf-8">
<title>Title</title>
</head>
<body>
</body>
</html>
```

Example HTML Document

Below is a well formed HTML 5 document that includes one comment and all the tags and text necessary for a web browser to draw the document. The document is shown drawn by the Google Chrome web browser in Figure 3-2.

Example 1

```
<!DOCTYPE HTML>
<html lang="en-us">
<head>
<!-- The following meta tag tells the browser that this document
     uses the 8-bit Unicode Transformation Format encoding. -->
<meta charset="utf-8">

<meta name="author" content="Rex Barzee">
<title>Horse Rentals</title>
</head>

<body>
<h1>Horse Rentals</h1>
<p>We rent horsies, big horsies, medium sized horsies, and little horsies (big
dogs really). Of course, this costs a great deal of money, and in order for us
to allow you to take the horsies anywhere, you must sign a lot of paper work,
about the same amount as if you were buying a house or being admitted to a
hospital (which might happen if you fall off one of our horsies).</p>

<p>We rent horsy saddles and other leather and metal stuff. Just ask for what
you want, and we probably have it. These are mostly used to control the horsies
which they don't like. If you don't take great care when putting these on the
horsies, you might be admitted to the hospital as mentioned in the above
paragraph.</p>

<p>We also rent horsy trailers. These trailers require a truck the size of Texas
that drinks diesel in order to actually pull them. Of course, if you don't have
a truck that fits this description, we'll rent you one. See the first paragraph
again for our rental terms (big money).</p>
</body>
</html>
```

Horse Rentals

We rent horsies, big horsies, medium sized horsies, and little horsies (big dogs really). Of course, this costs a great deal of money, and in order for us to allow you to take the horsies anywhere, you must sign a lot of paper work, about the same amount as if you were buying a house or being admitted to a hospital (which might happen if you fall off one of our horsies).

We rent horsy saddles and other leather and metal stuff. Just ask for what you want, and we probably have it. These are used mostly to control the horsies, which they don't like. If you don't take great care when putting these on the horsies, you might be admitted to the hospital as mentioned in the above paragraph.

We also rent horsy trailers. These trailers require a truck the size of Texas that drinks diesel in order to actually pull them. Of course, if you don't have a truck that fits this description, we'll rent you one. See the first paragraph again for our rental terms (big money).

Figure 3-2: An HTML document drawn in Google Chrome.

It is helpful to examine the tags in example 1 in more depth. How many different tags does example 1 use?
Seven. They are `<html>`, `<head>`, `<meta>`, `<title>`, `<body>`, `<h1>`, and `<p>`.

Which of those seven tags are void tags and have no closing tag?
`<meta>`.

Which of those seven tags have attributes?
`<html>` and `<meta>`.

Example HTML Document with a Form

The next example is a well formed HTML 5 document that includes all the tags and text necessary for a web browser to draw a document with two text fields, a text area, and two buttons. Even though this document is titled, "Send a Text Message" and it contains text fields and buttons, this document doesn't actually do anything. It doesn't do anything because it contains no `<script>` tags. A programmer adds functionality to an HTML document by writing JavaScript code between opening and closing `<script>` tags. Beginning in the next chapter, you will learn to write JavaScript code.

The document from example 2 is shown drawn by the Google Chrome web browser in Figure 3-3.

Example 2

```
<!DOCTYPE HTML>
<html lang="en-us">
<head>
<!-- The following meta tag tells the browser that this document
     uses the 8-bit Unicode Transformation Format encoding. -->
<meta charset="utf-8">
<meta name="author" content="Rex Barzee">
<title>Send a Text Message</title>
</head>

<body>
<h1>Send a text message</h1>
<p>From (your 10-digit wireless phone number):
<input type="text" id="txtFrom" size="10">
</p>
<p>To (10-digit wireless phone number):
<input type="text" id="txtTo" size="10">
</p>
<p>Message:<br>
<textarea id="txaMessage" rows="8" cols="40">
</textarea>
</p>
<p><button type="button">Send</button>
<button type="button">Clear</button>
</p>
</body>
</html>
```

Figure 3-3: An HTML document that contains text fields and buttons drawn by Google Chrome.

It is helpful to examine the tags in example 2 in more depth. How many different tags does example 2 use?

Eleven. They are `<html>`, `<head>`, `<meta>`, `<title>`, `<body>`, `<h1>`, `<p>`, `<input>`, `<br>`, `<textarea>`, and `<button>`.

Which of those 11 tags are void tags and have no closing tag?
`<meta>`, `<input>`, and `<br>`.

Which of those 11 tags have attributes?
`<html>`, `<meta>`, `<input>`, `<textarea>`, and `<button>`.

Notice that the two `<input>` tags and the `<textarea>` tag have an attribute named id. An id attribute uniquely identifies an element within an HTML document. In other words, the value for an id attribute must be unique within a document. Notice that the values for all three of the id attributes are different: id="txtFrom", id="txtTo", id="txaMesssage".

Notice that the two `<button>` tags have an attribute named onclick. The onclick attribute tells the browser what to do when a user clicks on a button. In the next chapter, you will use the onclick attribute to connect a button to JavaScript code. Then when a user clicks the button, the browser will execute that JavaScript code.

Does example 2 include a comment?
Yes, in the head there is a comment that describes the `<meta>` tag.

Common Mistakes

Forgetting to terminate a tag

Incorrect
```
<div Idaho, with its volcanic
soils and cool nights, is ideal
for growing potatoes.</div>
```

Correct
```
<div>Idaho, with its volcanic
soils and cool nights, is ideal
for growing potatoes.</div>
```

Forgetting the double quotes for an attribute

Incorrect
```
<div id="output></div>
```

Correct
```
<div id="output"></div>
```

Forgetting a closing tag

Incorrect
```
<b>really
```

Correct
```
<b>really</b>
```

Improperly nesting tags

Incorrect
```
<div>The average lifespan for a
female grizzly bear is estimated
at <b>26 years.</div></b>
```

Correct
```
<div>The average lifespan for a
female grizzly bear is estimated
at <b>26 years</b>.</div>
```

Forgetting to save an HTML file with a suffix of .html

In order for a browser to detect that your file is an HTML file, you must save it with a suffix of `.html`

Chapter Summary

- Hypertext markup language (HTML) is a computer language that is used to write documents.
- HTML 5 is the most recent version of HTML.
- An HTML 5 document must begin with a document type declaration and must contain a head and a body.
- HTML is composed of many tags. Each tag begins with a less than symbol (<) and ends with a greater than symbol (>).
- HTML tags usually come in pairs, an opening tag and a closing tag.
- Opening tags may contain attributes which are key/value pairs separated by the equal symbol (=).
- Opening tags that do not require a matching closing tag are called void tags.
- HTML tags should be properly nested.
- HTML is not case sensitive, so tags and attribute keys may be written in upper or lower case or any combination of upper and lower case.

Review Questions

1. What version of HTML is taught in this book?

2. Write the HTML 5 document type declaration as it should appear at the top of all HTML 5 documents. Include the surrounding less than (<) and greater than (>) symbols in your answer.

3. What is the first tag in an HTML 5 document? Include the surrounding less than (<) and greater than (>) symbols in your answer.

4. What are the two main sections that every HTML 5 document must have?

5. Inside which of the two main sections does the `<title>` tag belong?

6. What is the tag to begin the largest style of heading? Include the surrounding less than (<) and greater than (>) symbols in your answer.

7. What is the tag to begin a paragraph? Include the surrounding less than (<) and greater than (>) symbols in your answer.

8. Write the HTML tag and its attributes for creating a text field. Include the surrounding less than (<) and greater than (>) symbols in your answer.

9. Write the opening HTML tag and its attributes for creating a button. Include the surrounding less than (<) and greater than (>) symbols in your answer.

10. What is the attribute that a programmer can use to uniquely identify each element within an HTML document?

11. What are the characters that begin an HTML comment?

12. What is the tag that ends an HTML document? Include the surrounding less than (<) and greater than (>) symbols in your answer.

Assignments

1. Create and validate a well formed HTML 5 document that tells a short version of your life story. The document must include at least one heading and two paragraphs.

2. Create and validate a well formed HTML 5 document that advertises a business that you own or would like to start. The document must include at least one heading and two paragraphs.

3. Create and validate a well formed HTML 5 document that contains two text fields, a button, and a div. The text fields and the div must each have a unique id attribute.

Chapter 4. JavaScript Basics

JavaScript was originally developed by Brendan Eich at Netscape under the name Mocha, later renamed LiveScript, and finally renamed JavaScript. JavaScript is most often used in web pages on the client side (web browser). Despite its name, JavaScript has very little in common with the Java programming language. The little that they have in common includes the syntax of the C programming language and some naming conventions and names, such as Date, Math, and String. You can find a good online tutorial for JavaScript w3schools.com and a good online reference for JavaScript at developer.mozilla.org

Chapter Outcomes

By the end of this chapter, you will be able to:

- Read and write simple JavaScript programs embedded inside HTML documents.
- Write a JavaScript program that the computer runs when a user clicks a button.
- Write a JavaScript program that gets input from a popup window and sends output to a popup window.
- Write a JavaScript program that gets input from a text field and sends output to an HTML div.

Starting with JavaScript

Using your text editor, you can write JavaScript code in an HTML file. However, you must place the JavaScript code between opening and closing <script> tags as shown in example 1. Although it is possible to place <script> tags in the body of an HTML document, you should normally place <script> tags in the head of your HTML document. The HTML document from example 1 is shown drawn by the Google Chrome web browser in Figure 4-1.

Example 1

```
1   <!DOCTYPE HTML>
2   <html lang="en-us">
3   <head>
4   <meta charset="utf-8">
5   <title>My First JavaScript Program</title>
6   <script>
7   /* Defining Table
8    * Input: No user input
9    * Processing: None
10   * Output: The message "Water is delicious!"
11   */
12  function showMessage() {
13      // The next line of code causes the computer
14      // to open a popup window that contains the
15      // words "Water is delicious!"
16      alert("Water is delicious!");
17  }
```

```
18  </script>
19  </head>
20
21  <body>
22      <button type="button" onclick="showMessage()">Message</button>
23  </body>
24  </html>
```

Notice at line 22 in example 1 there are opening and closing button tags that create the button shown in Figure 4-1. Notice at line 22 that the button has an onclick attribute. When a user clicks this button, the computer executes the JavaScript code contained in the onclick attribute. The onclick code executes the showMessage function, which begins at line 12 and ends at line 17. Within this function at line 16 is a command, which causes the computer to open a popup window that contains the text "Water is delicious!" as shown in Figure 4-2.

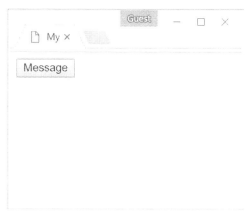

Figure 4-1: A simple HTML document with a single button drawn in Google Chrome.

To run the program in example 1, simply type all the code shown in example 1 (or copy and paste the code if you are reading this as an e-book) into a text editor. Do not type or copy the line numbers. Save the file with the suffix of .html, load the file in a browser, and click the Message button.

Running a Program

The computer runs or executes JavaScript code when certain events happen. These events include when an HTML document is loaded, when a user clicks a button, or even when a user moves the mouse. For example, the computer executes the function in example 1 when a user clicks the Message button.

Figure 4-2: A popup window that was opened by the Chrome browser because a user clicked the Message button.

Comments

A **comment** in a JavaScript program is a note or documentation that a programmer writes for himself or other programmers who will look at his code. The computer ignores comments. There are two styles of comments in JavaScript: single line and multi-line. A single line comment begins with two forward slashes (//), and ends at the end of the line of text. A multi-line comment begins with a forward slash and an asterisk (/*), and ends with an asterisk and a forward slash (*/). When writing a multi-line comment, many programmers start each line with an asterisk to make the comment stand out from the other code. Both styles of comments are shown in example 1, multi-line at lines 7–11 and single line at lines 13–15.

Statements

A JavaScript program is composed of statements. A **statement** is a complete command within a program. Statements in JavaScript end with a semicolon (;). Notice in example 1 that the statement at line 16 ends with a semicolon. When writing a program, a programmer will often group statements together in a **block** by surrounding the statements with curly braces: { and }.

Case Sensitive

JavaScript is **case sensitive**, so if you want your JavaScript program to work, you must be careful to always type characters with the correct case. For example, to cause the computer to open a popup window, you must type alert not Alert.

Declaring Variables

A **variable** is a location within the computer's memory to store data. When writing a computer program, a programmer declares variables so that the computer will reserve space in memory for the variables' contents. In JavaScript, we declare a variable by writing the keyword var and the variable's name. Here are several examples of declaring variables in JavaScript.

```
var price;
var numStudents;
var name;
```

String Concatenation

Within a JavaScript program, a piece of text is called a **string** of text. In JavaScript, you must surround all strings of text with quotes. It doesn't matter if you use single (') or double (") quotes, but you must be consistent. If you begin a string with a single quote then you must end it with a single quote. If you begin with double quotes, you must end with double quotes.

To create a large string of text from smaller strings of text you can use the **string concatenation** operator, which is the plus symbol (+). For example:

```
var name = "Samantha";
var message = "Hello, " + name + ". How are you today?";
```

Popup Windows

A JavaScript program can get user input by opening a popup window where a user can type input. Example 2 and Figure 4-3 contain an HTML document with a JavaScript program that

1. gets input from a user with a popup window
2. creates a greeting using string concatenation
3. displays that greeting to the user in another popup window

Example 2

```
1   <!DOCTYPE HTML>
2   <html lang="en-us">
3   <head>
4   <meta charset="utf-8">
5   <title>A Program to Say Hello</title>
6   <script>
7   /* Defining Table
8    * Input: A person's name
9    * Processing: Create a greeting for that person
10   * Output: The greeting
11   */
12  function greetUser() {
13      // This line prompts the user to type in his name.
14      var name = prompt("Please enter your name");
15
16      // Create a personalized greeting for the user.
17      var greeting = "Hello " + name + ". I hope you are well today.";
18
19      // The next line causes the computer to display
20      // a greeting to the user in a popup window.
21      alert(greeting);
22  }
23  </script>
24  </head>
25
26  <body>
27      <button type="button" onclick="greetUser()">Hello</button>
28  </body>
29  </html>
```

Programming Fundamentals in JavaScript

The program in example 2 works like this:

1. A user clicks the Hello button.
2. The program executes the code in the onclick attribute of the Hello button.
3. The onclick attribute causes the computer to execute the code in the greetUser function.
4. Line 14 causes the computer to open a popup window, which prompts the user to enter her name.
5. After the user enters her name, line 17 causes the computer to create a personalized greeting for the user.
6. Then line 21 causes the computer to display the greeting in another popup window.

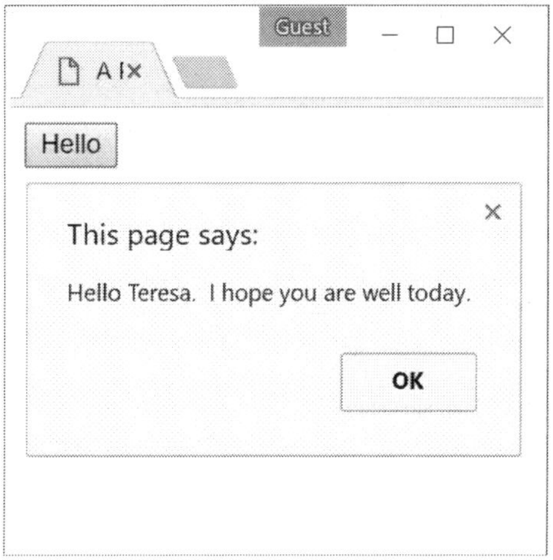

Text Fields and Divisions

A JavaScript program can also get input from text fields within a document and send output to a div. Using text fields and divs for input and output is better than using popup windows because popup windows annoy most users. Example 3 and Figure 4-4 show a program that uses a text field for input and a div for output. Recall from Chapter 3 that a div is simply a division or a part of an HTML document.

To get input from a text field, write an HTML document that contains a text field as shown on line 30 of example 3. Give the text field an id attribute. Each id within an HTML document must be unique. In other words, no other element in the HTML document is allowed to have the same id.

Figure 4-3: A simple JavaScript program that uses a popup window to ask a user for her name and then displays a greeting to that user.

After adding a text field to your document, write a JavaScript function like the one that begins at line 12. Within that function, write code that uses the built-in JavaScript function getElementById and the text field's id and value attributes to get the user's input as shown on line 15.

To send output to a div, first add a div with a unique id to your document as shown on line 32. Then as shown on line 24, add code to your function that uses the div's id and innerHTML attributes to store the results from your function in the div. Although it may seem strange and inconsistent, for a text field, you must use its value attribute, and for a div, you must use its innerHTML attribute. This is because the developers of HTML and JavaScript designed the value attribute to store what the user types in a text field. They designed the innerHTML attribute to hold what a user sees inside a div.

Example 3

```
1   <!DOCTYPE HTML>
2   <html lang="en-us">
3   <head>
4   <meta charset="utf-8">
5   <title>Applied Scripture</title>
6   <script>
7   /* Defining Table
8    * Input: A person's name
9    * Processing: Create a verse of scripture for that person
10   * Output: The scripture
11   */
12  function applyScripture() {
13      // Get the user's name from the text field that has the id
14      // of "nameInputBox" and store it in a variable named name.
15      var name = document.getElementById('nameInputBox').value;
16
17      // Use string concatenation to create a verse
18      // of scripture personalized for the user.
19      var scripture = "I, " + name + ", having been born of" +
20          " goodly parents, therefore I was taught somewhat" +
21          " in all the learning of my father.";
22
23      // Display the scripture in the div that has the id "outputDiv".
24      document.getElementById('outputDiv').innerHTML = scripture;
25  }
26  </script>
27  </head>
28
29  <body>
30  Please enter your name: <input type="text" id="nameInputBox">
31  <button type="button" onclick="applyScripture()">Verse</button>
32  <div id="outputDiv"></div>
33  </body>
34  </html>
```

The program in example 3 works like this:

Figure 4-4: A program to create a personalized verse of scripture.

1. A user enters his name in the text field.
2. A user clicks the Verse button.
3. The program executes the code in the onclick attribute of the Verse button.
4. The onclick attribute causes the computer to execute the code in the applyScripture function.
5. Line 15 causes the computer to read the user's name from the text field.
6. Line 19 cause the computer to create a personalized verse of scripture for the user.
7. Then line 24 causes the computer to display the verse in a div for the user to see.

Programming Fundamentals in JavaScript

The rules of HTML 5 require that the value of each id attribute be unique within a document. In addition, an id attribute cannot be empty and cannot contain spaces. In this book, we will use only English letters (A–Z and a–z) and Arabic digits (0–9) in the value of an id. For example:

```
<input type="text" id="salesInputBox">
<div id="output"></div>
```

Reserved Words

The following is a list of all reserved words in JavaScript. You should not use any of these words as variable or function names in your JavaScript programs.

JavaScript Keywords

break	case	catch	continue
debugger	default	delete	do
else	false	finally	for
function	if	in	instanceof
let	new	null	return
switch	this	throw	true
try	typeof	undefined	var
while	with		

JavaScript Types

Array	Boolean	Date	Function
Math	Number	Object	RegExp
String			

JavaScript Objects

document	event	window

JavaScript Unused but Reserved Words

abstract	boolean	byte	char
class	const	double	enum
export	extends	final	float
goto	implements	import	int
interface	long	native	package
private	protected	public	short
static	super	synchronized	throws
transient	void	volatile	yield

Fixing a Program that Doesn't Work

After you have finished writing a JavaScript program, if it isn't working, do the following to find and fix the problems.

1. Make sure you saved your HTML file with the suffix .html
2. Validate your HTML file by uploading it to the online validator at validator.w3.org
3. Load your HTML document in a web browser and check the JavaScript console for errors. You can view the console in Google Chrome by pressing Shift-Ctrl-J (Windows and Linux) or Command-Option-J (Mac).
4. Click the button in your HTML document to execute your code and check the JavaScript console again for errors.
5. Use the JavaScript debugger that is built into your web browser to step through your code line by line and watch the values of the variables.

Common Mistakes

Misspelling onclick

Incorrect
```
<button type="button" onlick="funcName()">
```
Correct
```
<button type="button" onclick="funcName()">
```

Leaving the onclick attribute of a button empty

Incorrect
```
<button type="button" onclick="">
```
Correct
```
<button type="button" onclick="funcName()">
```

Forgetting the parentheses after the function name in the onclick attribute

Incorrect
```
<button type="button" onclick="funcName">
```
Correct
```
<button type="button" onclick="funcName()">
```

Chapter Summary

- Within an HTML document, JavaScript programs must be placed inside script tags.
- To cause a computer to execute a JavaScript program when a user clicks a button, the button must have an onclick attribute.
- A JavaScript program may get input from a popup window or from a text field.
- A JavaScript program may send output to a popup window or to an HTML div.
- To make a large string of text from smaller strings of text, use the string concatenation operator which is the plus symbol (+).

Review Questions

1. What is the HTML tag that begins a section of JavaScript code? Include the surrounding less than (<) and greater than (>) symbols in your answer.

2. What is the JavaScript keyword to declare a variable?

3. What does the `document.getElementById` function do?
   a. display a message in a pop-up window and get input from a user
   b. find an element within an HTML document
   c. convert a number to text
   d. convert text to a number

4. What is the symbol that causes the computer to perform string concatenation?

5. Write the HTML tag that makes a text field that can be used by this JavaScript statement:

   ```
   var addr = document.getElementById('address').value;
   ```

   Include the surrounding less than (<) and greater than (>) symbols and necessary attributes in your answer.

6. Write the opening HTML tag to put a button in an HTML document. Include the surrounding less than (<) and greater than (>) symbols in your answer.

7. What is the attribute of a button that contains JavaScript code that will be executed when a user clicks on that button?

8. Write the opening HTML tag that makes a div that can be used by this JavaScript statement:

   ```
   document.getElementById('output').innerHTML = heartRate;
   ```

   Include the surrounding less than (<) and greater than (>) symbols and necessary attributes in your answer.

Programming Assignments

1. Type in the HTML and JavaScript code for example 2 in this chapter. Modify the code by changing the greeting that is displayed to the user. The changed greeting must include the user's name. Validate the code and load it in a web browser to run and test it.

2. Type in the HTML and JavaScript code for example 3 in this chapter. Modify the code by changing the scripture that is displayed to the user. Your program may display any scripture you want except 1 Nephi 1:1. The changed scripture must include the user's name. Validate the code and load it in a web browser to run and test it.

3. Create and validate a well formed HTML 5 document that you can use as a template for future assignments. At a minimum, your template must contain all the tags that are required in an HTML 5 document as explained in the "Required Tags" section of Chapter 3. In addition, your template must contain an opening script tag, a closing script tag, at least one input tag, an opening button tag, a closing button tag, an opening div tag, and a closing div tag.

4. Write an HTML 5 document that contains five text fields, a button, and a div. Write and test a JavaScript program that reads user input from all five text fields and concatenates all the input into one address and outputs the address in the div as shown in Figure 4-5.

Figure 4-5: An HTML document and JavaScript program that accepts input from five text fields, combines the input into one address, and outputs the address to a div.

Chapter 5. Variables and Arithmetic

A computer program is composed of data and instructions. The data may be temporarily stored in the computer's memory, or it may be stored more permanently on the computer's hard drive, a DVD, or a jump drive. When data is in the computer's memory, it is stored inside variables. A **variable** has a name, type, value, and scope. The term variable comes from the fact that a variable's value can be changed or varied.

Chapter Outcomes

By the end of this chapter, you will be able to:

- Declare a variable and assign a value to that variable.
- Write JavaScript code to copy the value from one variable to another variable.
- Write code to perform calculations and store the result in a variable.
- Use the increment and decrement operators in an arithmetic expression.
- Use the mathematical functions in the Math object.

Declaring a Variable

Before you can use a variable in a computer program, you must declare that variable. Declaring a variable tells a computer to reserve space in main memory for that variable. To declare a variable in a JavaScript program, simply write the keyword var and the variable's name. A variable name must start with an uppercase or lowercase letter, the underscore (_), or the dollar sign ($). The rest of the name must be made of letters, digits (0–9), the underscore, or the dollar sign. A variable name cannot include spaces. A variable name should be meaningful and should curtly describe what the variable stores. A computer programmer uses a variable's **name** in a program as a representation of the variable's **value**. This is similar to how a variable is used in an algebraic equation.

Template

```
var name, name2, name3...;
```

[handwritten: let name, name2, name3; →]

[handwritten: const = constant]

[handwritten: → block scoping { only works in the }]

Example 1

Declare three variables named x, balance, and interest.

```
var x;
var balance, interest;
```

Example 2

Declare two variables named roomNumber and occupants.

Variable Types

Each variable has a **type** so that the computer knows what kind of data can be stored in the variable and what operations the computer may perform on the variable. A variable in a JavaScript program may have any one of these types.

JavaScript Variable Types

Type	Purpose	Example
boolean	stores true or false	`true`
number	a number with or without a decimal point	`74.3`
string	a string of text	`"San Diego"`
function	a part of a program created using the keyword function	`function () { return 27; }`
object	an object such as an Array or Date	`{name:"Sam", phone:"1788"}`

ParseFloat(   ) makes a string into a number type

Assigning to a Variable

A programmer may assign a value to a variable at any point in a JavaScript program by using the assignment operator, which is simply the equal symbol (=). The assignment operator works from right to left, copying the value that is on the right side of the equal symbol and storing it into the variable or location that is on the left side of the equal symbol.

Template

```
name = value;
```

Example 3

Declare three variables named price, discRate, and title. Assign 12.95 and 0.25 to the first two variables and the text "A Poor Wayfaring Man of Grief" to the third variable.

```
var price, discRate;
var title;

price = 12.95;
discRate = 0.25;
title = "A Poor Wayfaring Man of Grief";
```

The computer determines a variable's type by the data that is stored in the variable. Notice that to store a number in a variable you must type the number without quotes around it, for example:

```
price = 12.95;
```

To store a string of text in a variable, you must put quotes (either double or single) around the text, for example:

```
title = "A Poor Wayfaring Man of Grief";
```

To store a boolean value in a variable, you must type either true or false in all lower case letters and without quotes, for example:

```
registered = false;
```

In JavaScript, the default value for all variables is undefined. If a programmer does not use the equal symbol (=) to assign a value to a variable, the value of that variable will be undefined, not 0, not null, but literally the value undefined. Obviously, undefined is not a number and cannot be successfully used as part of a calculation. To help ensure that all variables have a value other than undefined, the JavaScript language allows a programmer to assign a value to a variable when it is declared. This is sometimes called **initializing** a variable, and many programmers like it because it saves the programmer from writing an extra line of code.

Template

```
var name = value, name2 = value2, name3 = value3…;
```

Example 4

Declare a variable named price and assign the number 12.95 to it. Also, declare a variable named title and assign the text "A Poor Wayfaring Man of Grief" to it.

```
var price = 12.95;
var title = "A Poor Wayfaring Man of Grief";
```

Example 5

Declare a variable named occupants and assign the value 3 to it.

Desk Checks

While reading the rest of this book, you will find it helpful to step through the example code line by line as if you were a computer. Doing this is sometimes called a **desk check** because you are checking the code on paper or "at your desk" instead of running it on a computer. To perform a desk check, draw a table that represents part of the computer's main memory. Step through the given code line by line as if you were the computer, and change the value of each variable just as the computer would. For example, if you were given the following code:

```
1   var x = 7;
2   var y = -3;
3   var a = x;
4   x = 4;
```

You would draw a table like this to represent part of the computer's main memory.

Desk Check

x	y	a
~~7~~	–3	7
4		

Notice that the first line of the code changes the value of the variable x to 7, so in the table 7 is written underneath the heading "x". The second line of code changes y to -3, so -3 is written underneath "y". The third line of code copies the value of x into a, so 7 is written underneath "a". Finally, the last line of code changes the value of x to 4, so 7 is crossed through and 4 is written below "x".

Technically, writing one value beneath another, as shown in the desk check table for x, does not accurately model the way a computer stores a value in a variable. When the computer assigns a new value to a variable, it replaces the old value with the new value. To model this accurately in a desk check, we would erase the old value and replace it with the new value. However, to understand how code works, it is often helpful to see a history of the values that a variable has held over time, so when you complete the desk checks, you should cross through an old value and write a new value below the old one.

Sometimes example code requires input from the user or somewhere else. This input is given in the desk check table. For example, the code:

```
var y = x;
```

requires that the variable x already have a value. This value will be given in the desk check table:

Desk Check

x	y
15	

Swapping Values

If a program needs to exchange the value of one variable with another variable, or in other words swap their values, a common and easy way to do this is to use a temporary variable. The example code below uses a temporary variable named *swap* to exchange the values of two variables: a and b. Desk check this code. To perform a desk check, step through the example code line by line as if you were a computer and write the value for each variable in the empty boxes. A missing box is a hint that means there is no value for you to write in that spot.

Example 6

```
var swap = a;
a = b;
b = swap;
```

Desk Check

a	b	swap
8	-3	

Programming Fundamentals in JavaScript

Arithmetic Expressions

The word computer comes from the ability these machines have to compute values or in other words to perform arithmetic. A programmer tells the computer to perform arithmetic by writing arithmetic expressions in a program. An **arithmetic expression** is composed of **operands** (numbers and variables) and **operators** (addition, multiplication, etc.).

Arithmetic in JavaScript is written differently than it is written in algebra. For example in algebra, $3x$ ~~means~~ to multiply 3 times x. However, typing 3x in a JavaScript program will not cause the computer to multiply anything. Instead, it will simply cause an error. If you want multiplication in JavaScript, you must use the multiplication operator (*) like this: 3 * x.

Arithmetic Operators

The five basic arithmetic operations that a computer can perform are multiplication, division, modulus, addition, and subtraction. As explained earlier in this chapter, a computer can also assign a value to a variable. A programmer makes the computer perform these arithmetic operations by writing the corresponding operator (symbol) in a program. Here are the arithmetic operators available in JavaScript.

JavaScript Arithmetic Operators

Operator	Name	Algebraic Expression	JavaScript Expression
−	negation	$-r$	-r
*	multiplication	vt or $v \cdot t$ or $v \times t$	v * t
/	division	$x \div y$ or x / y	x / y
%	modulus	$r \bmod s$	r % s = remainder
+	addition	$p + q$	p + q
−	subtraction	$f - 3$	f − 3
=	assignment	$s = t$	s = t

Modulus

The **modulus** operator is sometimes called the remainder operator because it returns the remainder after division. However, its correct name is the modulus operator because it returns the **signed** remainder after division, which means the remainder can be positive or negative. In JavaScript, the sign of a modulus result depends only on the sign of the dividend (operand on the left of the %).

Examples

```
  7  %   3  =   1
 12  %   3  =   0
 −6  %   4  =  −2
  6  %  −4  =   2
 −6  %  −4  =  −2
```

In addition to the basic arithmetic operators, most computer languages provide functions to compute exponentiation, square root, logarithms, sine, cosine, and others.

Operator Precedence

When an arithmetic expression includes two or more different operators, the result is often ambiguous. For example, what is the result of $7 - 3 * 2$? Is it 8 or 1? The answer depends on the order in which the arithmetic operations are done. Because of this ambiguity, programming languages include arithmetic operator **precedence**. Precedence determines which operator the computer evaluates first and which it evaluates last.

JavaScript Arithmetic Operator Precedence

Operator(s)	Name(s)	Precedence
( )	parentheses	Highest (evaluated first)
−	negation	
* / %	multiplication, division, modulus	
+ −	addition, subtraction	
=	assignment	Lowest (evaluated last)

When an expression includes two operators with the same precedence, the computer evaluates them from left to right. For example, in the arithmetic expression x / y * c, the computer will first divide *x* by *y* then multiply that result by *c*. When writing an arithmetic expression, if you need a lower precedence operator evaluated before a higher precedence one, you can add parentheses to change the evaluation order. The computer will always evaluate arithmetic that is inside parentheses first regardless of the operator precedence.

Example 7

Translate the algebraic equation $v = i \left(1 + \dfrac{a}{n}\right) \dfrac{y}{n}$ into JavaScript.

```
var v = i * (1 + a / n) * (y / n);
```

Example 8

Translate the algebraic equation $x = \dfrac{7}{2(r + 13)} - 3(a + bc)$ into JavaScript.

Celsius to Fahrenheit

The formula for converting a temperature in Celsius to Fahrenheit is $f = \dfrac{9}{5}c + 32$

Example 9 is a JavaScript program that uses this formula to convert a temperature entered by a user in Celsius to a temperature in Fahrenheit. Notice at line 14 of example 9 the program contains code to read the value that a user typed into a text field and to store that value in a variable named text. At line 17, the parseFloat function converts what the user typed from a string into a number. Line 17 is necessary because a computer always treats values typed by a user as if they were text. This is true no matter what the user types. If a user clicks in a text field and then presses the 5 key and then the 8 key, a human will look at the user input and think of it as the number 58, but a computer will treat it as the digit "5" followed by the digit "8". In other words, if you are writing a program to get user input and to perform calculations with that input, then your program must convert the user input from a string of text into a number before performing calculations with that number. Converting from text to a number is what the parseFloat function does as shown on line 17.

Example 9

```
1   <!DOCTYPE HTML>
2   <html lang="en-us">
3   <head>
4   <meta charset="utf-8">
5   <title>Convert Celsius to Fahrenheit</title>
6
7   <script>
8   /* Input: a temperature in Celsius
9    * Processing: convert the temperature from Celsius to Fahrenheit
10   * Output: the temperature converted to Fahrenheit
11   */
12  function celsToFahr() {
13      // Read a Celsius temperature from the user.
14      var text = document.getElementById('celsiusInputBox').value;
15
16      // Convert what the user typed from text into a number.
17      var c = parseFloat(text);
18
19      // Convert the Celsius temperature into Fahrenheit.
20      var f = c * 9 / 5 + 32;
21
22      // Display the Fahrenheit temperature to the user.
23      document.getElementById('fahrenDiv').innerHTML = f;
24  }
25  </script>
26  </head>
27
28  <body>
29  Enter a temperature in Celsius: <input type="text" id="celsiusInputBox">
30  <button type="button" onclick="celsToFahr()">Convert</button>
31  <div id="fahrenDiv"></div>
32  </body>
33  </html>
```

Desk Check

text	c	c * 9	c * 9 / 5	f
"20"				

In JavaScript, there are two functions to convert a string of text into a number: parseInt and parseFloat. parseInt converts a string to an integer. If a user enters text with digits after the decimal point, parseInt will convert only the digits before the decimal point and will ignore the digits after the decimal point. For example, if a user enters "75.814", parseInt will convert that to the number 75. parseFloat converts a string to a number that may have digits after the decimal point. For example, parseFloat will convert the string "75.814" to the number 75.814 or a close approximation to 75.814.

Fahrenheit to Celsius

The formula for converting a temperature in Fahrenheit to Celsius is $\quad c = \dfrac{5}{9}(f - 32)$

In some programming languages, such as Java, C++, and C, this formula must be carefully written because in those languages 5 / 9 causes the computer to perform **integer division** which truncates the result by simply dropping the digits after the decimal point. Thus, in such languages 5 / 9 yields 0, and a programmer must write the code in a way to force the computer to perform floating-point division instead of integer division. However, in JavaScript, the division operator always causes the computer to perform floating-point division.

Example 10

```
<!DOCTYPE HTML>
<html lang="en-us">
<head>
<meta charset="utf-8">
<title>Convert Fahrenheit to Celsius</title>

<script>
/* Input: a temperature in Fahrenheit
 * Processing: convert the temperature from Fahrenheit to Celsius
 * Output: the temperature converted to Celsius */
function fahrToCels() {
    // Read a Fahrenheit temperature from the user.
    var text = document.getElementById('fahrenInputBox').value;

    // Convert what the user typed from text into a number.
    var f = parseFloat(text);

    // Convert the Fahrenheit temperature into Celsius.
    var c = 5 / 9 * (f - 32);

    // Display the Celsius temperature to the user.
    document.getElementById('celsiusDiv').innerHTML = c;
 }
</script>
</head>

<body>
Enter a temperature in Fahrenheit: <input type="text" id="fahrenInputBox">
<button type="button" onclick="fahrToCels()">Convert</button>
<div id="celsiusDiv"></div>
</body>
</html>
```

Desk Check

text	f	f − 32	5 / 9	c
"25"				

Assignment Operators

In addition to the arithmetic operators described above, JavaScript also has assignment operators that perform arithmetic. These operators are really shortcuts for performing arithmetic using the current value of a variable and then storing the result of the arithmetic back into that variable.

JavaScript Assignment Operators

Operator	Name	Example	Equivalent Expression
*=	multiplication assignment	x *= 5;	x = x * 5;
/=	division assignment	s /= t;	s = s / t;
%=	modulus assignment	w %= z;	w = w % z;
+=	addition assignment	x += y;	x = x + y;
-=	subtraction assignment	r -= t;	r = r - t;

For example, x += 2 is equivalent to x = x + 2. In other words the += operator is a combination of addition and assignment and is a shortcut way of writing a command with both. Here are some interesting uses of the assignment operators and some equivalent statements. Understanding these examples will help you better understand the assignment operators.

Example 11

```
x += x;
// 1. retrieve the value in x
// 2. add the value in x to it
// 3. store the sum back in x
```

Equivalent Example

```
x *= 2;
// 1. retrieve the value in x
// 2. multiply that value by 2
// 3. store the sum back in x
```

Example 12

```
x -= x;
// 1. retrieve the value in x
// 2. subtract the value in x from it
// 3. store the difference back in x
```

Equivalent Example

```
x = 0;
// store 0 in x
```

Example 13

```
x *= -1;
// 1. retrieve the value in x
// 2. multiply that value by -1
// 3. store the product back in x
```

Equivalent Example

```
x = -x;
// change the sign of x
```

Imagine a program to compute the price of a pizza. The price of a large sized cheese pizza with no other toppings is $10.95. The price for each topping such as ham, peperoni, olives, and pineapple is $1.45. Here is a short example that uses the += operator to compute the price of a pizza.

Example 14

```
var price = 10.95;
var toppings = 3;
var perTopping = 1.45;
price += toppings * perTopping;
```

Desk Check

price	toppings	perTopping
~~10.95~~	3	1.45
15.30		

Now imagine a program to compute sales tax and the total amount that a customer owes. The next three examples show three different ways that a program could compute the total including sales tax that a customer owes.

Example 15

```
var subtotal = 175;
var tax = subtotal * 0.06;
var total = subtotal + tax;
```

Desk Check

subtotal	tax	total
175	10.5	185.5

Example 16

```
var total = 175;
var tax = total * 0.06;
total += tax;
```

Desk Check

total	tax
~~175~~	10.5
185.5	

Example 17

```
var total = 175;
total *= 1.06;
```

Desk Check

total
~~175~~
185.5

Increment and Decrement Operators

JavaScript includes two more shortcut operators called the increment and decrement operators. The increment operator (++) simply adds one to the value of a variable. The decrement operator (--) subtracts one from the value of a variable.

JavaScript Increment and Decrement Operators

Operator	Name	Example	Equivalent Expressions
++	pre-increment	++x;	x += 1; x = x + 1;
	post-increment	x++;	
--	pre-decrement	--t;	t -= 1; t = t - 1;
	post-decrement	t--;	

Both the increment and decrement operators can be written as a pre or post operator. If you write one of these operators before a variable name, such as ++x, then it is a pre-increment, meaning the computer will perform the increment *before* the rest of the arithmetic in the same statement. If you write one of the operators after a variable name, such as x++, then it is a post-increment, meaning the computer will perform the increment *after* the rest of the arithmetic in the same statement. However, if you use the increment or decrement operator in a statement all by itself, then it makes no difference whether you use the pre or post version. The next two examples show how pre and post-increment work when written inside a larger statement.

Example 18

```
var a = 4;
var b = ++a * 3 + 2;
```

Desk Check

a	b
~~4~~	17
5	

Example 19

```
var a = 4;
var b = a++ * 3 + 2;
```

Desk Check

a	b
~~4~~	14
5	

Notice in example 18, line 1 causes the computer to store the number 4 in the variable *a*. On line 2, because the increment operator is written as a pre-increment, the computer first adds 1 to the value of *a*, and then performs the rest of the calculations on line 2 which results in 17 being stored in the variable *b*.

In example 19, line 1 causes the computer to store the number 4 in the variable *a*. On line 2, because the increment operator is written as a post-increment, the computer first performs the other calculations on line 2 which results in 14 being stored in *b*, and then increments the value of *a* from 4 to 5. Notice in example 19 that incrementing *a* does not affect the value of *b* because the increment is a post-increment and the computer increments *a* after calculating the value of *b*.

When a new programmer first understands the post-increment operator, the most common question she asks is "Why? Why would anyone ever use the post-increment operator to change the value of a variable after the other calculations in the same statement are done?" The answer is "to prepare the incremented variable (*a* in examples 18 and 19) to be used later in the program."

When writing the increment or decrement operator, remember that it makes no difference whether you write the pre or post version of the operators if the operator is in a statement all by itself. For example:

```
a++;
```

Here are three more examples of using the increment and decrement operators.

Example 20

```
var x = 3;
var y = ++x * 2 + 5;
```

Desk Check

x   y

Example 21

```
var x = 3;
var y = x++ * 2 + 5;
```

Desk Check

x   y

Example 22

```
var q = 7;
var s = 2 + 18 / --q;
```

Desk Check

q   s

Operator Precedence Revisited

The following table shows the precedence for all the JavaScript arithmetic operators shown in this chapter.

JavaScript Arithmetic Operator Precedence

Operator(s)	Name(s)	Precedence
( )	parentheses	Highest (evaluated first)
−	negation	
++ --	increment, decrement	
* / %	multiplication, division, modulus	
+ −	addition, subtraction	
= += −= *= /= %=	assignment operators	Lowest (evaluated last)

Remember that the pre-increment is always executed before the rest of the arithmetic in the same statement, and the post-increment, even though it has a higher precedence, is always executed after the rest of the arithmetic in the same statement.

Math Object

The Math object is an object (see chapter 11) built into JavaScript that enables a program to perform more advanced mathematical computations. It contains the following mathematical constants and functions, all of which must be preceded by "Math." when you use them in a program.

ALWAYS CAPITALIZED

Math Object Constants

Constant	Description	Algebraic Expression	Approximate Value
E	Euler's number	e	2.71828
LN2	Natural logarithm of 2	$\ln 2$	0.69315
LN10	Natural logarithm of 10	$\ln 10$	2.30259
LOG2E	Base-2 logarithm of Euler's number	$\log_2 e$	1.44270
LOG210	Base-10 logarithm of Euler's number	$\log_{10} e$	0.43429
PI	Ratio of a circle's circumference to its diameter	π	3.14159
SQRT1_2	Square root of ½	$\sqrt{½}$	0.70711
SQRT2	Square root of 2	$\sqrt{2}$	1.41421

Math Object Functions

Function	Description
abs(x)	absolute value of x
acos(x)	arccosine of x in radians
asin(x)	arcsine of x in radians
atan(x)	arctangent of x as a numeric value in the range $[-\pi/2, \pi/2]$ radians
atan2(y, x)	arctangent of the quotient of its arguments
ceil(x)	smallest integer that is larger than or equal to x
cos(x)	cosine of an angle x (x is in radians)
exp(x)	Euler's number raised to the power of x (e^x)
floor(x)	largest integer that is smaller than or equal to x
log(x)	natural logarithm of x ($\ln x$)
max(x, y, z...)	largest value of many numbers
min(x, y, z...)	smallest value of many numbers
pow(y, x)	y raised to the power of x (y^x)
random()	a pseudo random number in the range [0.0, 1.0)
round(x)	integer that is nearest x
sin(x)	sine of an angle x (x is in radians)
sqrt(x)	square root of x
tan(x)	tangent of an angle x (x is in radians)

Volume of a Cylinder

If we know the radius and length of a cylinder, we can compute the volume of that cylinder using the formula: $v = \pi r^2 h$ where v is the volume, r is the radius, and h is the length of the cylinder. This formula can be written in JavaScript as shown in the next example. Notice the use of the built-in JavaScript constant `Math.PI` at line 18.

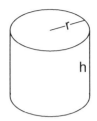

Figure 5-1: A cylinder with radius r and height h.

Example 23 contains a program that reads the *radius* and *height* for a cylinder from a user, and then computes and outputs the volume for that cylinder. Notice the code at line 14 combines into a single line, the code to read text from a text field and the code to convert that text into a number. In previous programs, these two steps were written separately like this:

```
var text = document.getElementById('radiusInput').value;
var r = parseFloat(text);
```

In example 23, these two steps are combined by wrapping `parseFloat` around the code to get the input, like this:

```
var r = parseFloat(document.getElementById('radiusInput').value);
```

Combining these two steps into one line of code is convenient for a programmer and reduces the number lines of code. In fact, in example 23, there are two lines of code, lines 14 and 15 that combine the get input step and the convert step.

Example 23

```
1  <!DOCTYPE HTML>
2  <html lang="en-us">
3  <head>
4  <meta charset="utf-8">
5  <title>Volume</title>
6
7  <script>
8  /* Input: radius and height of a cylinder
9   * Processing: Calculate the volume of the cylinder.
10  * Output: the volume
11  */
12 function volume() {
13     // Get the radius and height from the user.
14     var r = parseFloat(document.getElementById('radiusInput').value);
15     var h = parseFloat(document.getElementById('heightInput').value);
16
17     // Compute the volume of the cylinder.
18     var v = Math.PI * r * r * h;
19
20     // Display the volume to the user.
21     document.getElementById('outputDiv').innerHTML = v;
22 }
23 </script>
24 </head>
25
26 <body>
27 Radius <input type="text" id="radiusInput" size="5"><br>
28 Height <input type="text" id="heightInput" size="5"><br>
29 <button type="button" onclick="volume()">Volume</button>
30 <div id="outputDiv"></div>
31 </body>
32 </html>
```

Desk Check

r	h	v
2.7	5	

Round to Decimal Places

The built in JavaScript Math object has a function named Math.round that rounds a real number to an integer. However, a programmer will occasionally need to write a program that rounds fractional numbers to a fixed number of places after the decimal point. For example, U.S. currency amounts are usually rounded to two decimal places (pennies). Lines 27–29 of the next example use the built in Math.pow and Math.round functions to round the value in the variable named *dist* to two decimal places.

Figure 5-2 shows a plot of two points in two-dimensional Cartesian space and the distance between those points. We can compute the distance between two points p_1 and p_2 with the formula:

$$d = \sqrt{(x_2 - x_1)^2 + (y_2 - y_1)^2}$$

where d is the distance between the points. Point p_1 has the coordinates (x_1, y_1), and point p_2 has the coordinates (x_2, y_2). This formula can be written in JavaScript as shown in the next example. Notice the use of the built-in JavaScript function Math.sqrt at line 24.

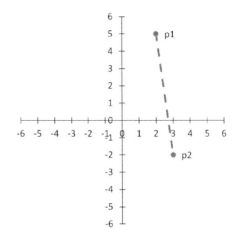

Figure 5-2: A plot of two points.

Example 24

```
1   <!DOCTYPE HTML>
2   <html lang="en-us">
3   <head>
4   <meta charset="utf-8">
5   <title>Distance</title>
6
7   <script>
8   /* Input: x and y for two points: x1, y1, x2, y2
9    * Processing:
10   *    1. Calculate the distance between the two points.
11   *    2. Round the distance to two digits after the decimal.
12   * Output: the rounded distance
13   */
14  function distance() {
15      // Get the coordinates for two points from the user.
16      var x1 = parseFloat(document.getElementById('x1inputBox').value);
17      var y1 = parseFloat(document.getElementById('x2inputBox').value);
18      var x2 = parseFloat(document.getElementById('y1inputBox').value);
19      var y2 = parseFloat(document.getElementById('y2inputBox').value);
20
21      // Compute the distance between the two points.
22      var dx = x2 - x1;
23      var dy = y2 - y1;
24      var dist = Math.sqrt(dx * dx + dy * dy);
25
26      // Round the distance to two digits after the decimal.
27      var digits = 2;
28      var multiplier = Math.pow(10, digits);
29      dist = Math.round(dist * multiplier) / multiplier;
30
31      // Display the distance to the user.
32      document.getElementById('outputDiv').innerHTML = dist;
33  }
34  </script>
35  </head>
36
37  <body>
38  Please enter the x and y coordinates for two points:<br>
39  (x1, y1) <input type="text" id="x1inputBox" size="3">
40           <input type="text" id="y1inputBox" size="3"><br>
41  (x2, y2) <input type="text" id="x2inputBox" size="3">
42           <input type="text" id="y2inputBox" size="3"><br>
43  <button type="button" onclick="distance()">Distance</button>
44  <div id="outputDiv"></div>
45  </body>
46  </html>
```

Desk Check

x1	y1	x2	y2	dx	dy	dist	digits	multiplier
7	−2	4	6					

Common Mistakes

[handwritten: Stick w/ let]

Forgetting to declare a variable

Incorrect
```
 miles = 61;
```
Correct
```
  var miles = 61;
```

Declaring the same variable twice

Incorrect
```
 var total = 175;
 var total *= 1.06;
```
Correct
```
  var total = 175;
  total *= 1.06;
```
[handwritten: once declared - dont do it again]

Forgetting quotes around text

Incorrect
```
 var speaker = Monson;
```
Correct
```
  var speaker = 'Monson';
  // or
  var speaker = "Monson";
```

Forgetting to convert (parse) text to a number

Incorrect
```
 var x = document.getElementById('num1').value;
 var sum = x + 5;
```

Correct
```
 var x = parseInt(document.getElementById('num1').value);
 var sum = x + 5;
```
[handwritten: removes decimal - use parseFloat]

Using caret (^) for exponentiation

Incorrect
```
 var g = (1 + r) ^ n;
```
Correct
```
  var g = Math.pow(1 + r, n);
```

Using parentheses for multiplication

Incorrect
```
 var z = 3(x + y);
```
Correct
```
  var z = 3(*)(x + y);
```

Programming Fundamentals in JavaScript

Chapter Summary

- Before using a variable in JavaScript, you must declare it. To declare a variable, write the keyword var followed by the variable's name.
- Use the assignment operator (=) to assign a value to a variable.
- Within a JavaScript program, use these operators: *, /, %, +, - to multiply, divide, compute the remainder after division, add, and subtract.
- The assignment operators (*=, /=, %=, +=, -=) are shortcuts for performing arithmetic using the current value of a variable and then storing the result into that variable.
- To add one to the value of a variable, you can use the increment operator (++). You can use the decrement operator (--) to subtract one from the value of a variable.
- Each of the arithmetic operators has a precedence. It is important that you understand precedence when writing formulas in JavaScript.
- To program a computer to perform more advanced arithmetic, such as exponentiation, square root, and rounding, you must use the functions in the Math object.

Review Questions

1. Declare two variables named balance and rate.

2. Declare a variable named inventor and assign the text "Franklin" to it.

3. In JavaScript what does the keyword var do?
   a. reserve space in the computer's memory for a variable
   b. store a value in a variable
   c. convert a number to text
   d. prompt the user for input

4. What does the parseInt function do?
   a. display a message in a pop-up window
   b. display a message in a pop-up window and get input from a user
   c. convert an integer to text
   d. convert text to an integer

5. What does the parseFloat function do?
   a. display a message in a pop-up window
   b. display a message in a pop-up window and get input from a user
   c. convert a number to text
   d. convert text to a number

6. After a computer executes the following JavaScript code, variable *a* will be of what data type?

   ```
   var a = false;
   ```

7. After a computer executes the following JavaScript code, variable *b* will be of what data type? Hint: pay attention to the double quotes.
```
var b = "true";
```

8. After a computer executes the following JavaScript code, variable *c* will be of what data type?
```
var c = 15;
```

9. After a computer executes the following JavaScript code, variable *e* will be of what data type and hold what value?
```
var c = 15;
var d = -2.17;
var e = c + d;
```

10. After a computer executes the following JavaScript code, variable *h* will be of what data type and hold what value?
```
var f = "Her name is ";
var g = "Isabella";
var h = f + g;
```

11. After a computer executes the following JavaScript code, variable *k* will be of what data type?
```
var i = document.getElementById('number1').value;
var j = document.getElementById('number2').value;
var k = i + j;
```

12. After a computer executes the following JavaScript code, variable *p* will be of what data type?
```
var m = parseInt(document.getElementById('number1').value);
var n = parseFloat(document.getElementById('number2').value);
var p = m + n;
```

13. After a computer executes the following JavaScript code, variable *r* will be of what data type and hold what value?
```
var c = 15;
var r = "You found " + c + " coins.";
```

14. Write a JavaScript statement to calculate the amount of energy released during a nuclear reaction. In other words, translate $E = mc^2$ into JavaScript. Assume that the variables *m* and *c* already exist and that each holds a value. When writing your answer, be sure to declare *E* and use the variable names given in the equation above.

15. The semi-perimeter, *s*, of a triangle with side lengths *a*, *b*, and *c* is given by the formula:
$$s = \frac{a + b + c}{2}$$

Translate this formula into JavaScript. Assume that the variables *a*, *b*, and *c* already exist and that each holds a value. When writing your answer, be sure to declare *s* and use the variable names given in the equation above.

16. Translate this formula into JavaScript.
$$r = 2k + \frac{6 - n}{3p^2}$$
Assume that the variables k, n, and p already exist and that each holds a value. When writing your answer, be sure to declare r and use the variable names given in the equation above.

17. Rewrite the following JavaScript statement so that it doesn't use the += operator but still has the same functionality.
```
z += x - 3 * y;
```
Assume that the variables x, y, and z already exist and that each holds a value. When writing your answer, be sure to use the variable names given in the statement above.

18. Rewrite the following JavaScript statement so that it doesn't use the *= operator but still has the same functionality.
```
b *= q - s;
```
Assume that the variables b, q, and s already exist and that each holds a value. When writing your answer, be sure to use the variable names given in the statement above. Hint: pay close attention to operator precedence.

Programming Assignments

1. Write a defining table and a JavaScript program that asks a user for a volume in quarts and then converts that value into liters. Your program should correctly handle real numbers such as 7.54.

2. Write a defining table and a JavaScript program that asks a user for a distance in kilometers and then converts that value into miles. Your program should correctly handle real numbers.

3. An employee at a grocery store must frequently place boxes of cans in stacks. Write a defining table and a program that allows him to enter the total number of boxes and the number of boxes he will place in each stack. Your program must output the number of stacks he will have to make. All of the stacks except the last one must have the exact number of boxes that the employee specifies. The last stack must have the exact number or fewer boxes. For example, if the employee enters 74 total boxes and 6 boxes in each stack your program must output 13.

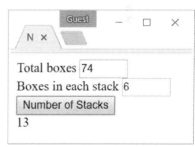

4. A teacher frequently divides her class into teams. Write a defining table and a program that allows her to enter the number of students in her class and the number of teams she wants. The number of members on each team must be as balanced as possible. In other words, if not all of the teams can have the same number of members then some of the teams will have only one more member than the other teams. Your program must output a phrase that tells the teacher how to divide her class into teams. For example, if the teacher entered 22 class members and 5 teams, your program must output "2 teams with 5 members and 3 teams with 4 members." Your program must list the larger teams first.

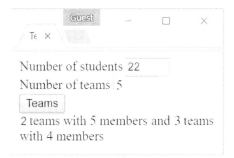

5. Write a defining table and a JavaScript program to compute the mileage of a vehicle. Your program should allow the user to enter the beginning and ending odometer readings and the number of gallons of gasoline used and should output the mileage in miles per gallon. Your program should correctly handle real numbers.

6. When you exercise to strengthen your heart, you should maintain your heart rate within a range. To find that range, subtract your age from 220. This difference is your maximum heart rate per minute. Your heart simply will not beat faster than this maximum (220 – age). When exercising to strengthen your heart, you should keep your heart rate between 65% and 85% of your heart's maximum. Write a defining table and a JavaScript program that asks for a person's age and computes and outputs the slowest and fastest rates necessary to strengthen his heart.

7. Write a defining table and a JavaScript program to compute and output an employee's after tax pay. Your program will read from the keyboard the number of regular hours that an employee worked and that employee's wage, and then compute that employee's after tax pay. Tax is 15% of the employee's gross pay. Your program should correctly handle real numbers.

8. The length of a cable can be approximated with this formula:
$$L = s + \frac{8d^2}{3s}$$
where L is the length of the cable, s is the distance that the cable must span, and d is the distance the cable will sag or dip. Write a defining table and a program that allows a user to enter the distance a cable must span and the distance the cable will sag. Your program must compute and output the length of the cable.

9. The size of a car tire in the United States is represented with three numbers like this: 205/60R 15. The first number is the width of the tire in millimeters. The second number is the aspect ratio. The third number is the diameter in inches of the wheel that the tire fits. Write a defining table and a program that reads from the keyboard those three numbers for a tire and computes and outputs the volume of space inside that tire. The volume of space inside a tire can be approximated with this formula:

$$v = \frac{\pi w^2 a(wa + 2{,}540d)}{10{,}000{,}000}$$

where v is the volume in cubic centimeters, w is the width of the tire in millimeters, a is the aspect ratio of the tire, and d is the diameter of the wheel in inches. Hint: the Math object contains a constant named Math.PI.

Guest — □ ×

Ti ×

Tire Width (mm): 205
Aspect Ratio: 60
Wheel Diameter (in): 15

Volume (cm³)
39924.5

Chapter 6. Selection

In order for computer programs to be useful, a computer must be able to make decisions. The computer makes decisions by evaluating a condition and if the condition is true, selecting one set of statements to execute. If the condition evaluates to false, then the computer selects a different set of statements to execute. This decision making ability is known as **selection** because the computer is selecting either one group of statements or another group of statements to execute. A selection statement is also called an **if statement** because in most programming languages it starts with the keyword if.

Chapter Outcomes

By the end of this chapter, you will be able to read and write:

- if statements with a single condition
- nested if statements
- a set of if…else if…else statements
- switch statements which can be used instead of a set of if…else if…else statements

Relational Operators

A selection statement always has a **condition**, which is the test the computer uses to select one set of statements or the other. A condition always evaluates to either true or false. Any expression that evaluates to either true or false is called a **boolean** expression named after the British mathematician George Boole. There are six JavaScript **relational operators**, which test the relation between two values and yield only true or false.

JavaScript Relational Operators

Operator	Name	Example
<	less than	if (i < 3)
>	greater than	if (x > y)
<=	less than or equal to	if (row <= end)
>=	greater than or equal to	if (age >= 8)
==	equal to	if (col == last)
!=	not equal to	if (col != last)

The relational operators are used inside the condition of selection statements. Shown below are the different forms of selection statements available in JavaScript.

if ...

Use when:

- A true choice exists and the false choice does not exist

Template

```
if (condition) {
    statements;
}
```

When the computer executes the condition, if the condition evaluates true, then the computer executes the statements inside the body of the `if` statement. Otherwise the computer skips the statements in the body of the `if` statement.

Example 1

```
if (balance > 500) {
    var interest = balance * 0.03;
    balance += interest;
}
document.getElementById('outputDiv').innerHTML = balance;
```

Figures 6-1 and 6-2 show the order in which the computer will execute the statements from example 1. Figure 6-1 shows that when *balance* is greater than 500, the computer will execute the statements inside the body of the `if` statement. Figure 6-2 shows that when *balance* is not greater than 500, the computer will skip the statements inside the body of the `if` statement.

```
            true
if (balance > 500) {

    var interest = balance * 0.03;
    balance += interest;
}
document.getElementById('outputDiv').innerHTML = balance;
```

Desk Check

balance	interest
~~700~~	21
721	

Figure 6-1: When *balance* is greater than 500, the computer will execute the statements inside the body of the `if` statement.

```
            false
if (balance > 500) {

    var interest = balance * 0.03;
    balance += interest;
}
document.getElementById('outputDiv').innerHTML = balance;
```

Desk Check

balance	interest
300	

Figure 6-2: When *balance* is not greater than 500, the computer will skip the statements inside the body of the `if` statement.

if ... else ...

Use when:

- A true and a false choice exists

Template

```
if (condition) {
    statements;
}
else {
    statements;
}
```

When the computer executes the condition, if the condition evaluates true, then the computer executes the statements inside the body of the if statement and skips the statements in the body of the else clause. Otherwise the computer skips the statements in the body of the if statement and executes the statements in the body of the else clause. The else clause is optional as shown in the previous section.

Example 2

```
var bonus;
if (sales <= 1000) {
    bonus = 20;
}
else {
    bonus = 100;
}
var salary = sales * 0.10 + bonus;
```

Figures 6-3 and 6-4 show the order in which the computer will execute the statements from example 2. Figure 6-3 shows that when *sales* is less than or equal to 1000, the computer will execute the statements inside the body of the if statement and skip the statements in the else. Figure 6-4 shows that when *sales* is greater than 1000, the computer will skip the statements inside the body of the if statement and execute the statements in the else.

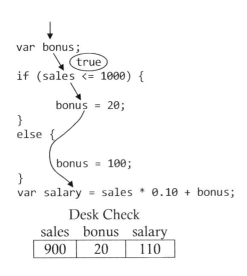

Desk Check

sales	bonus	salary
900	20	110

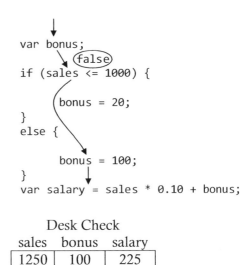

Desk Check

sales	bonus	salary
1250	100	225

Figure 6-3: When *sales* is less than or equal to 1000, the computer will execute the statements inside the body of the if statement and skip the statements in the else.

Figure 6-4: When *sales* is greater than 1000, the computer will skip the statements inside the body of the if statement and execute the statements in the else.

Programming Fundamentals in JavaScript

if ... else if ... else ...

Use when:
- More than two choices exist
- Each choice is based on different variables or uses an operator other than equals (==)

Template

```
if (condition) {
    statements;
}
else if {
    statements;
}
...
else {
    statements;
}
```

When a group of `if` statements is connected using `else`, the computer evaluates the conditions one at a time until one of them evaluates true. The computer executes the statements inside the first `if` that evaluates true and skips all other statements. If none of the conditions evaluates true, the computer executes the statements in the last `else` clause only. The last `else` clause is optional as are all the `else` clauses.

Example 3

```
var discount;
if (cost < 100) {
    discount = 0.10;
}
else if (cost < 250) {
    discount = 0.15;
}
else if (cost < 400) {
    discount = 0.18;
}
else {
    discount = 0.20;
}
cost *= (1 - discount);
```

Figures 6-5, 6-6, and 6-7 show the order in which the computer will execute the statements from example 3. Figure 6-7 shows that when *cost* is less than 100, the computer will execute the statements inside the body of the first if statement and skip the statements in the else statements. Figure 6-6 shows that when *cost* is between 250 and 400, the computer will skip the statements inside the body of the first two if statements, execute the statements in the body of the third if statement, and then skip the last else. Figure 6-5 shows that when *cost* is greater than 400, the computer will skip the statements inside the bodies of the first three if statements and execute the code in the body of the last else.

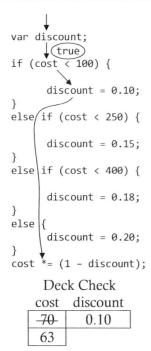

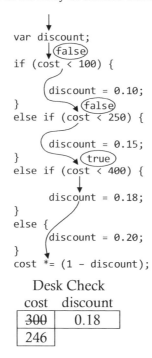

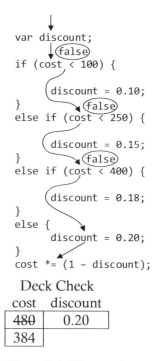

Figure 6-7: When *cost* is less than 100, the computer will execute the statements inside the body of the first if statement and skip the statements in the else statements.

Figure 6-6: When *cost* is between 250 and 400, the computer will skip the statements inside the body of the first two if statements, execute the statements in the body of the third if statement, and then skip the last else.

Figure 6-5: When *cost* is greater than 400, the computer will skip the statements inside the bodies of the first three if statements and execute the statements in the body of the last else.

Power of else

Many beginning programmers forget that the keyword else can be used by itself without another if statement. For example, when writing an if statement that will execute different code for males and females, many beginning programmers write something like this:

Programming Fundamentals in JavaScript

```
if (gender == 'M') {
    // Code for males goes here.
}
else if (gender == 'F') {
    // Code for females goes here.
}
```

The second if statement, if (gender == 'F'), is unnecessary and simply clutters the code and makes more work for the computer. Instead, that code example should be written like this:

```
if (gender == 'M') {
    // Code for males goes here.
}
else {
    // Code for females goes here.
}
```

Notice that the keyword else can be used by itself. When used in this way, the equivalent in English is "everything else." Consider this example code that gives a 40% discount to minors, no discount to adults, and a 25% discount to senior citizens.

```
var rate;
if (age < 18) {
    // Code for minors goes here.
    rate = 0.4;
}
else if (age < 58) {
    // Code for adults goes here.
    rate = 0;
}
else if (age < 100) {
    // Code for senior citizens goes here.
    rate = 0.25;
}
```

In this age example, the third if statement is not only unnecessary, it is also awkward. What age should we write in the third if statement? At what advanced age should the program stop considering someone a senior citizen? There isn't a good answer to this question. Instead, the correct way to write this code is to remove the last if statement and allow the else, by itself, to mean "everyone else."

```
var rate;
if (age < 18) {
    // Code for minors goes here.
    rate = 0.4;
}
else if (age < 57) {
    // Code for adults goes here.
    rate = 0;
}
else {
    // Code for senior citizens goes here.
    rate = 0.25;
}
```

switch

Use when:
- More than two choices exist
- Each choice is based on the same variable and uses equals (==)
- Comparison values are integer or string

Template

```
switch (variable) {
    case constValue1:  statements;  break;
    case constValue2:  statements;  break;
    ...
    default: statements;  break;
}
```

(handwritten annotation:) ★ — w/out it will run all within { } kind of like an "or" w/the if

A `switch` statement functions like a group of connected `if` ... `else if` ... `else` statements that all test one variable for equality. When the computer executes a `switch` statement, it compares the value of the variable in the parentheses with each case one at a time. The computer skips statements for the cases that do not equal the value of the variable. It executes the statements after the first case that equals the value of the variable *and* continues executing statements in the `switch` until it encounters a break statement or the `switch` ends whichever happens first. If none of the cases equals the value of the variable, the computer skips the statements in all cases and executes the statements in the `default` case until it encounters a break or the `switch` ends. The `default` case is optional.

Example 4

```
var registerDate;
switch (classStanding) {
    case 'F':
        registerDate = "Nov 23";
        break;
    case 'S':
        registerDate = "Nov 17";
        break;
    case 'J':
        registerDate = "Nov 12";
        break;
    case 'N':
        registerDate = "Nov 6";
        break;
    default:
        registerDate = "none";
        alert("unknown class standing");
        break;
}
document.getElemenById('outputDiv').innerHTML = registerDate;
```

Desk Check

classStanding	registerDate
'F'	"Nov 23"

Desk Check

classStanding	registerDate
'J'	"Nov 12"

Desk Check

classStanding	registerDate
'Q'	"none"

Even Integers

The easiest way for a computer to determine if an integer is even is to divide the number by two, and if the remainder of this division is equal to zero, then the integer is even. The modulus operator performs integer division and returns the signed remainder of the division. The code example below uses the modulus operator to determine if an integer is even.

Example 5

```
<!DOCTYPE HTML>
<html lang="en-us">
<head>
<meta charset="utf-8">
<title>Is Even?</title>

<script>
/* Input: An integer
 * Processing: Determine if the integer is even or odd
 * Output: A message that says the integer is even or odd
 */
function isEven() {
    // Get the user input from a text field and convert it to a number.
    var text = document.getElementById('integerInputBox').value;
    var value = parseInt(text);

    // Choose a message.
    var message;
    if ((value % 2) == 0) {
        message = value + " is an even integer";
    }
    else {
        message = value + " is an odd integer";
    }

    // Display the message to the user.
    document.getElementById('outputDiv').innerHTML = message;
}
</script>
</head>

<body>
Please enter an integer: <input type="text" id="integerInputBox">
<button type="button" onclick="isEven()">Is Even?</button>
<div id="outputDiv"></div>
</body>
</html>
```

↘ converts to # (handwritten annotation)

Desk Check (handwritten annotation)

text	value	value % 2	message
"8"			

Odd Integers

Because the result of the modulus operator is signed, when determining if an integer is even or odd the result of the modulus operator must always be compared to zero. Comparing the result to one will *not* work for negative, odd integers. Consider this JavaScript code and two corresponding desk checks.

Example 6

```
// Wrong! Doesn't work for negative odd integers!
if ((number % 2) == 1) {
    document.getElementById('outputDiv').innerHTML = number + ' is odd';
}
else {
    document.getElementById('outputDiv').innerHTML = number + ' is even';
}
```

Desk Check		
number	number % 2	output
5	1	"5 is odd"

Desk Check		
number	number % 2	output
−9	−1	"−9 is even"

Notice that comparing (value % 2) == 1 works fine for positive integers whether they are even or odd. However, as shown in the desk check above, it does *not* work for negative, odd integers. If you need to write code that takes action only if an integer is odd, the correct way to write the comparison is with the not equal relational operator (!=)

Example 7

```
// Correct check for odd integers
if ((value % 2) != 0) {
    document.getElementById('outputDiv').innerHTML = value + ' is odd';
}
```

Sometimes a programmer will use the bitwise And (&) operator to test if an integer is even as shown below. Such code works but is a bad solution for at least two reasons.

- It is not as straight forward as using the modulus operator.
- It depends on the computer using two's complement, binary representation for integers. (Admittedly, computers will continue to represent integers using two's complement for the foreseeable future.)

Example 8

```
// Correct, but poor check for even integers!
if ((value & 1) == 0) {
    document.getElementById('outputDiv').innerHTML = value + ' is even';
}
```

Programming Fundamentals in JavaScript

Many programmers write a test for even integers using the bitwise And operator because it may execute faster than a test using the modulus operator. However, the disadvantages of such code, almost never justify the very small, possible gain in execution speed, especially because most modern compilers will automatically optimize the compiled version of the statement using the modulus operator: if ((value % 2) == 0) to be the same as using the bitwise And operator: if ((value & 1) == 0)

Quadratic Formula

A quadratic equation of the form $y = ax^2 + bx + c$ has two solutions, also called roots, that may or may not be distinct and that may be real or complex. If you graph a quadratic equation, the roots are the locations where the equation crosses the x-axis. Figure 6-8 contains the graph of three different quadratic equations. Notice that the first equation (on the left) crosses the x-axis twice and therefore has two real roots. The second equation crosses or touches the x-axis only once and therefore has only one distinct real root. The third equation does not cross the x-axis and so its two roots are **complex**

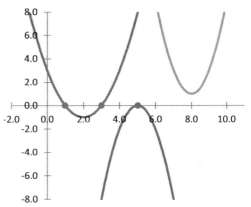

Figure 6-8: A graph of three quadratic equations.

meaning they contain the square root of -1. The square root of -1 does not exist, and mathematicians say it is **imaginary**.

We can find the roots of a quadratic equation by using the quadratic formula:

$$x = \frac{-b \pm \sqrt{b^2 - 4ac}}{2a}$$

Within the quadratic formula, $b^2 - 4ac$ is called the discriminant because it discriminates between equations that have two, one, or zero real roots. If the discriminant is positive (greater than zero), then the equation has two real roots. If the discriminant is zero, then the equation has only one root, and it is a real root. If the discriminant is negative (less than zero), then the roots include the square root of -1 and are complex.

Here is JavaScript code for finding the real roots of a quadratic equation if they exist. Notice the if statement that uses the discriminant to determine if the roots exist (are real) or do not exist (are complex).

Example 9

```html
<!DOCTYPE HTML>
<html lang="en-us">
<head>
<meta charset="utf-8">
<title>Quadratic Formula</tille>

<script>
/* Input: Three coefficients from a quadratic equation.
 * Processing: If they exist, compute the root or roots of the equation
 * Output: The root or roots of the equation or
 *          "undefined" if they don't exist.
 */
function quadratic() {
    // Get three coefficients a, b, and c
    // for a quadratic equation from the user.
    var a = parseFloat(document.getElementById('aInputBox').value);
    var b = parseFloat(document.getElementById('bInputBox').value);
    var c = parseFloat(document.getElementById('cInputBox').value);

    // Compute the root or roots of the quadratic equation if they exist.
    var discr = b * b - 4 * a * c;
    var root1, root2;
    if (discr >= 0) {
        var sq = Math.sqrt(discr);
        root1 = (-b + sq) / (2 * a);
        root2 = (-b - sq) / (2 * a);
    }

    document.getElementById('outputDiv').innerHTML = root1 + ' ' + root2;
}
</script>
</head>

<body>
y = <input type="text" id="aInputBox" size="3"> x<sup>2</sup> +
    <input type="text" id="bInputBox" size="3"> x +
    <input type="text" id="cInputBox" size="3">
<button type="button" onclick="quadratic()">Compute Roots</button>
<div id="outputDiv"></div>
</body>
</html>
```

Desk Check

a	b	c	discr	sq	root1	root2
1	−4	3				

Programming Fundamentals in JavaScript

Nested If Statements

It is often useful to write one `if` statement inside another `if` statement or inside the `else` part of an `if` statement. Consider the problem to write a program that reads from the keyboard the total weekly sales for a sales person and then outputs the sales person's commission according to this table.

If the sales amount is greater than or equal to	And the sales amount is less than	Then the commission rate is
0	$300	0%
$300	$600	2.0%
$600	$1000	2.5%
$1000	∞	3.0%

This can be easily written using nested `if` statements as shown in the following code example. Notice the `if` statements nested inside the `else` statements.

Example 10

```
var sales = parseFloat(document.getElementById('salesInputBox').value);
var rate;
if (sales < 300) {
    rate = 0;
}
else {
    if (sales < 600) {
        rate = 0.02;
    }
    else {
        if (sales < 1000) {
            rate = 0.025;
        }
        else {
            rate = 0.03;
        }
    }
}
var commission = sales * rate;
var output = 'The employee earned ' + commission;
document.getElementById('outputDiv').innerHTML = output;
```

Desk Check

sales	rate	commission	output
850			

Although the previous example is correct, it can be written in a slightly shorter way by combining the else and if statements like this.

Example 11

```
var sales = parseFloat(document.getElementById('salesInputBox').value);
var rate;
if (sales < 300) {
    rate = 0;
}
else if (sales < 600) {
    rate = 0.02;
}
else if (sales < 1000) {
    rate = 0.025;
}
else {
    rate = 0.03;
}
var commission = sales * rate;
var output = 'The employee earned ' + commission;
document.getElementById('outputDiv').innerHTML = output;
```

Desk Check

sales	rate	commission	output
850			

As another example, consider a sports team that wants to provide discounted tickets to students and senior citizens and that wants to reward loyal fans that attend multiple games according to this table.

Age	Games Attended	Ticket Price
0 – 17	0 – 5	$8.00
0 – 17	6 – 10	$6.00
0 – 17	11 and up	$5.00
18 – 54	0 – 10	$10.00
18 – 54	11 and up	$8.00
55 and older	0 – 10	$8.00
55 and older	11 and up	$6.00

This could also be solved using nested if statements as shown in the next example.

Example 12

```
<!DOCTYPE HTML>
<html lang="en-us">
<head>
<meta charset="utf-8">
<title>Ticket Price</title>

<script>
/* Input: A person's age and the number of games that person has attended
 * Processing: Determine the price to charge a person for a ticket to a game
 * Output: The ticket price */
function ticketPrice() {
    var age = parseInt(document.getElementById('ageBox').value);
    var gamesAttended = parseInt(document.getElementById('gamesBox').value);
    var price;
    if (age < 18) {
        if (gamesAttended < 6)
            price = 8.0;
        else if (gamesAttended < 11)
            price = 6.0;
        else
            price = 5.0;
    }
    else if (age < 55) {
        if (gamesAttended < 11)
            price = 10.0;
        else
            price = 8.0;
    }
    else {
        if (gamesAttended < 11)
            price = 8.0;
        else
            price = 6.0;
    }

    document.getElementById('priceDiv').innerHTML = price;
}
</script>
</head>

<body>
Age: <input type="text" id="ageBox" size="3"><br>
Number of games attended: <input type="text" id="gamesBox" size="3"><br>
<button type="button" onclick="ticketPrice()">Ticket Price</button>
<div id="priceDiv"></div>
</body>
</html>
```

Desk Check

age	gamesAttended	price
38	6	

Sometimes nested `if` statements can be a little tricky as shown in the following example which has two `if` statements but only one `else` statement. According to the rules of JavaScript, an `else` statement is paired with only one `if` statement. This means that in the example code below, if the first condition (x < 2) is true and the second condition (y > 8) is false, the computer will not change *message* to either "Hello" or "Goodbye". In that situation, the computer will display "Wave".

Example 13

```javascript
var message = 'Wave';
if (x < 2) {
    if (y > 8) {
        message = 'Hello';
    }
}
else {
    message = 'Goodbye';
}
document.getElementById('outputDiv').innerHTML = message;
```

Figures 6-9, 6-10, and 6-11 show the order in which the computer will execute the statements from example 13. Figure 6-9 shows that when *x* is less than 2 and *y* is greater than 8, the computer will change *message* to "Hello". Figure 6-10 shows that when *x* is not less than 2, the computer will change *message* to "Goodbye". Figure 6-11 shows that when *x* is less than 2 and *y* is not greater than 8, the computer will not change *message* to either "Hello" or "Goodbye". In that situation, *message* will remain "Wave" and the computer will display "Wave".

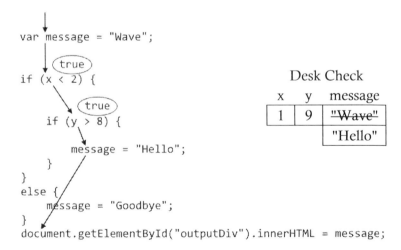

Figure 6-9: When *x* is less than 2 and *y* is greater than 8, the computer will change *message* to "Hello".

Programming Fundamentals in JavaScript

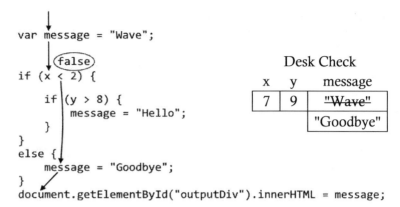

Figure 6-10: When *x* is not less than 2, the computer will execute the code in the matching `else` block which will change *message* to "Goodbye".

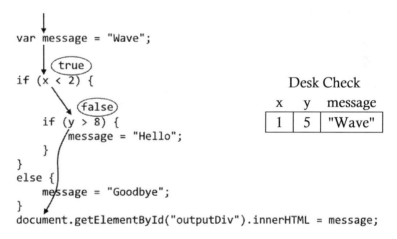

Figure 6-11: When *x* is less than 2 and *y* is not greater than 8, the computer will not execute the code in the `else` block because the `else` block is paired with the first `if` statement and the comparison in the first `if` statement is true. This means that in this situation the computer will not change *message* to "Hello" or "Goodbye" but will leave *message* as "Wave".

Common Mistakes

Forgetting parentheses around the condition

```
Incorrect           Correct
 if x < 7 {          if (x < 7) {
 }                   }
```

Using assignment instead of comparison

```
Incorrect            Correct
 if (age = 18) {      if (age == 18) {
 }                    }
```

Placing a semicolon at the end of an if statement

```
Incorrect                  Correct
 if (growth > 500); {       if (growth > 500) {
 }                          }
```

Placing a semicolon at the end of an else clause

```
Incorrect                 Correct
 if (growth > 500) {       if (growth > 500) {
 }                         }
 else; {                   else {
 }                         }
```

Forgetting braces when there is more than one statement inside an `if` statement

```
Incorrect                       Correct
 if (bal > 500)                  if (bal > 500) {
     var intr = bal * 0.03;          var intr = bal * 0.03;
     bal += intr;                    bal += intr;
                                 }
```

Adding a condition to an else clause

```
Incorrect                      Correct
 if (gender == 'F') {           if (gender == 'F') {
 }                              }
 else (gender == 'M') {         else {
 }                              }
```

Unnecessary Comparisons

```
Incorrect                  Correct
 if (age < 18) {            if (age < 18) {
 }                         }
 else if (age >= 18) {      else {
 }                         }
```

Chapter Summary

- Selection is a control structure that allows the computer to execute one group of statements and skip another group of statements.
- An if statement is a selection statement that begins with the JavaScript keyword if.
- An if statement must have a condition in parentheses. The parentheses contain code to compare two values.
- There are six comparison operators in JavaScript: equal to (==), not equal to (!=), less than (<), less than or equal to (<=), greater than (>), greater than or equal to (>=).
- A switch statement is a selection statement that begins with the JavaScript keyword switch and can be used instead of a long set of if … else if … else statements.

Review Questions

1. Write an if statement to determine if the value in the variable *age* is greater than 12.

2. Write an if statement to check if the value in the variable *x* is not equal to the value in the variable *y*.

3. Write an if statement that displays "go south" if the value in the variable *temperature* is less than 32, and displays "enjoy" otherwise.

4. Write an if statement that displays "replace tires" if the value in the variable *depth* is less than 0.16, and displays "enjoy" otherwise.

5. The following if statement contains an error. Rewrite it so that it is correct. Assume the variable *age* already exists and holds a valid number.
   ```
   if age < 8 {
   ```

6. The following if statement contains an error. Rewrite it so that it is correct. Assume the variable *age* already exists and holds a valid number.
   ```
   if (age = 21) {
   ```

7. The following if statement contains an error. Rewrite it so that it is correct. Assume the variable *age* already exists and holds a valid number.
   ```
   if (age >= 30); {
   ```

8. The following if statement contains an error. Rewrite it so that it is correct. Assume the variable *age* already exists and holds a valid number.
   ```
   if (age =< 55) {
   ```

9. Given the following JavaScript code, what will the computer output for the user to see?
```javascript
var x = 1, y = 7;
var message = "Welcome";
if (x < 2) {
    if (y > 10) {
        message = "Hello";
    }
}
else {
    message = "Goodbye";
}
alert(message);
```

10. Given the following JavaScript code, what will the computer output for the user to see?
```javascript
var x = 1, y = 7;
var message = "Welcome";
if (x < 2) {
    if (y > 10) {
        message = "Hello";
    }
    else {
        message = "Goodbye";
    }
}
alert(message);
```

Programming Assignments

1. Write a defining table and then a program that computes and outputs the absolute difference between two numbers entered by a user. In other words, your program should always show the difference as a positive number. Examples:

Numbers		Output
6	8	2
8	6	2
−3	5	8
5	−3	8
−7	−4	3

2. Write a defining table and a program that helps a user choose the correct foot wear for the day's weather. The following table shows the weather types the user may enter and what your program should output.

Weather	Foot Wear
hot	sandals
rain	galoshes
snow	boots

If the user enters any other weather type, your program should output "shoes".

3. Write a defining table and then a program that reads from the keyboard a student's name and number of completed university credits and then outputs the student's name and year in school according to this table.

If the number of credits is greater than or equal to	And the number of credits is less than	Then the year in school is
0	30	freshman
30	60	sophomore
60	90	junior
90	∞	senior

4. A bank will not loan money to a homebuyer unless the homebuyer pays for part of the house at the time of purchase. This initial payment is called a down payment and is based on the cost of the home. The Bank of Ririe calculates down payments according to this schedule:

Cost of House			Down Payment
$0	–	$49,999.99	5% * cost
$50,000	–	$99,999.99	$2,000 + 10% * (cost – $50,000)
$100,000	–	$199,999.99	$7,500 + 20% * (cost – $100,000)
$200,000	–	∞	$27,500 + 25% * (cost – $200,000)

For example a house that costs $126,900 would have a down payment of 7,500 + 20% * (126,900 – 100,000) = $12,880. Write a defining table and a program that gets the cost of a house from a user and calculates and outputs the down payment based on the Bank of Ririe's schedule.

5. A university library that loans books to students, faculty, and the public has a written policy that determines how long someone may borrow a book before it is due. This table shows the criteria and length of time that someone is allowed to borrow a book.

Patron Status	Number of Overdue Books in the Last Year	Loan Duration (weeks)
student	0	6
	fewer than 3	4
	3 or more	2
faculty	0	16
	fewer than 3	12
	3 or more	8
other	0	4
	fewer than 3	3
	3 or more	2

Write a defining table and a JavaScript program that determines how long a person may borrow a book. Your program must allow a librarian to enter a person's status: "student", "faculty", or "other" and how many books the person has kept past the due date in the last year.

6. Write a defining table and a program to quiz a child on simple arithmetic. The program should allow a child to enter two numbers and an arithmetic operator (+, −, *, or /) and the child's answer to the problem. The program should compute the correct answer and compare it to the child's answer and output "Correct! Good job." or "Incorrect. Try again!" The user interface for your program should look similar to Figure 6-12.

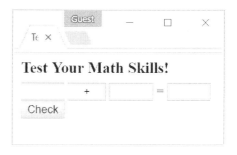

Figure 6-12: The user interface for a program to quiz children on arithmetic.

7. Roman numerals are still used today to display a year on the cornerstone of buildings. Write a defining table and then a program to convert a four digit decimal number into Roman numerals. The Roman number system has the digits

Roman	Arabic
I	1
V	5
X	10
L	50
C	100
D	500
M	1000

The rules for writing Roman numerals are

a. Thousands, hundreds, tens, and ones are written separately.
b. The numbers 1 to 9 are I, II, III, IV, V, VI, VII, VIII, IX
c. Tens are written the same way, except X, L, and C are used: X, XX, XXX, XL, L, LX, LXX, LXXX, XC
d. Hundreds are written the same way, except C, D, and M are used: C, CC, CCC, CD, D, DC, DCC, DCCC, CM
e. Thousands can be no larger than 3000 and are M, MM, MMM

As an example, 1987 is MCMLXXXVII (1000 = M, 900 = CM, 80 = LXXX, and 7 = VII).

Chapter 7. Logic

When writing a condition in an if statement, we often want the computer to evaluate more than one comparison. For example, we may want the computer to check if a person is male and older than forty years. To combine more than one comparison within an if statement we use the logical operators.

Chapter Outcomes

By the end of this chapter, you will be able to:

- Read and write if statements with multiple comparisons in the condition.
- Understand the logical operators: Not (!), And (&&), Inclusive Or (||), and Exclusive Or (^).
- Use the logical operators to refine online searches.
- Write truth tables to help you evaluate and rewrite logical expressions.

Logical Operators

To combine two or more comparisons in the condition of a single if statement, we use the logical operators, also called the boolean operators. The following table describes the four JavaScript logical operators.

JavaScript Logical Operators

Operator	Name	Description
!	Not	Unary operator that reverses or switches a false value to true and a true value to false.
&&	And	Binary operator that combines two conditions, and the combined condition is true, if and only if both conditions are true, otherwise the combined condition is false.
||	Inclusive Or (Or)	Binary operator that combines two conditions, and the combined condition is true, if either or both conditions are true, otherwise the combined condition is false.
^	Exclusive Or (Xor)	Binary operator that combines two conditions, and the combined condition is true, if and only if one condition is true and the other is false, otherwise the combined condition is false.

Notice that Inclusive Or is often abbreviated as Or, and Exclusive Or is often abbreviated as Xor. Notice also that Not (!) is a unary operator which means it operates on only one value, unlike And (&&), Or (||), and Xor (^) which are binary operators. Because Not is a unary operator, it has a higher precedence than the other logical operators.

Template

```
if (condition1 OPERATOR condition2) {
    statements;
}
```

Example 1

```
if (balance > 0 && daysSincePayment > 30) {
    balance += latePenalty;
}

if (sqft < 1500 || height > 30) {
    approved = false;
}
```

Choosing a Group

A programmer can use the logical operators to write code that chooses in which group a person or item belongs. Consider the following program that reads a girl's age from the keyboard and determines which class she should attend. The program uses these criteria to choose the correct class.

Age	Class
younger than 12	Primary
12 or 13	Beehive
14 or 15	Mia Maid
16 or 17	Laurel
18 or older	Relief Society

Example 2

```html
<!DOCTYPE HTML>
<html lang="en-us">
<head>
<meta charset="utf-8">
<title>Which Class</title>

<script>
/* Input: A girl's age
 * Processing: If statements to choose a class
 * Output: Name of the class
 */
function chooseClass() {
    var age = parseInt(document.getElementById('age').value);

    var group;
    if (age <= 11) {
        group = 'Primary';
    }
    else if (age == 12 || age == 13) {
        group = 'Beehive';
    }
    else if (age == 14 || age == 15) {
        group = 'Mia Maid';
    }
    else if (age == 16 || age == 17) {
        group = 'Laurel';
    }
    else if (age >= 18) {
        group = 'Relief Society';
    }

    document.getElementById('output').innerHTML = group;
}
</script>
</head>

<body>
Please enter your age: <input type="text" id="age" size="5"><br>
<button type="button" onclick="chooseClass()">Class</button>
<div id="output"></div>
</body>
</html>
```

Desk Check

age	group
14	

Each of the if statements for Beehive, Mia Maid, and Laurel uses the logical Inclusive Or operator and shows the correct way to write JavaScript code that determines if a variable holds one of two values. For example, this is the correct way to write JavaScript code to determine if a person's age is 12 or 13 years old:

```
if (age == 12 || age == 13) {
```

The next example contains a program that reads a boy's age from the keyboard and determines which scouting group he should attend. The program uses these criteria to choose the correct group.

Age	Group
7	Tiger
8	Wolf
9	Bear
10	Webelos
between 11 and 13, inclusive	Boy Scout
between 14 and 20, inclusive	Venture

Example 3

```
<!DOCTYPE HTML>
<html lang="en-us">
<head>
<meta charset="utf-8">
<title>Which Group</title>
<script>
/* Input: A boy's age
 * Processing: If statements to choose a group
 * Output: Name of the group
 */
function chooseGroup() {
    var age = parseInt(document.getElementById('age').value);

    var group;
    if (age < 7) {
        group = 'When you are 7 years old, you can become a Tiger Scout.'
    }
    else if (age == 7) {
        group = 'Tiger';
    }
    else if (age == 8) {
        group = 'Wolf';
    }
    else if (age == 9) {
        group = 'Bear';
    }
    else if (age == 10) {
        group = 'Webelos';
    }
    else if (11 <= age && age <= 13) {
        group = 'Boy Scout';
    }
    else if (14 <= age && age <= 20) {
        group = 'Venture';
    }
    else {
        group = 'You are too old to join scouting as a participant.'
            + ' Perhaps you would like to volunteer as a leader.';
    }
```

Desk Check

age	group
15	

```
      document.getElementById('output').innerHTML = group;
}
</script>
</head>

<body>
Please enter your age: <input type="text" id="age" size="5"><br>
<button type="button" onclick="chooseGroup()">Class</button>
<div id="output"></div>
</body>
</html>
```

The if statements for Boy Scout and Venture use the logical And operator and show the correct way to write JavaScript code that determines if the value in a variable falls within a range. For example, this is the correct way to write JavaScript code that determines if a person's age is between 14 and 20, inclusive:

```
      if (14 <= age && age <= 20) {
```

Disneyland Autopia

According to the Disneyland website, guests wishing to drive a car on the Autopia must meet one of the following height requirements:

- 54 inches (137 cm) or taller to drive alone
- 32 inches (81 cm) or taller and accompanied by a passenger 54 inches or taller

Here is a JavaScript program that accepts the height of a driver and an optional passenger and uses the logical operators || and && to determine if they may ride the Autopia. Notice the use of parentheses in the if statement to ensure the logic is correct. The program outputs either "Enjoy the ride!" or "Sorry, to drive a car on the Autopia you must be at least 54 inches tall or at least 32 inches tall and accompanied by a passenger who is at least 54 inches tall."

Example 4

```html
<!DOCTYPE HTML>
<html lang="en-us">
<head>
<meta charset="utf-8">
<title>Are you tall enough to drive on the Autopia?</title>

<script>
/* Input: the height of a driver and an optional passenger
 * Processing: Determine if a driver and
 *      optional passenger may ride the Autopia
 * Output: "Enjoy the ride!" or
 *      "Sorry, to drive a car on the Autopia you must be
 *      at least 54 inches tall or at least 32 inches tall and
 *      accompanied by a passenger who is at least 54 inches tall."
 */
function checkHeight() {
    var driver = parseInt(document.getElementById('driverBox').value);
    var passenger = parseInt(document.getElementById('passengerBox').value);

    var message;
    if (driver >= 54 || (driver >= 32 && passenger >= 54)) {
        message = 'Enjoy the ride!';
    }
    else {
        message = 'Sorry, to drive a car on the Autopia you must be ' +
                'at least 54 inches tall or at least 32 inches tall and ' +
                'accompanied by a passenger who is at least 54 inches tall.';
    }

    document.getElementById('outputDiv').innerHTML = message;
}
</script>
</head>

<body>
<h1>Are you tall enough to drive on the Autopia?</h1>
Driver's height in inches:
    <input type="text" id="driverBox" size="3"><br>
Passenger's height in inches:
    <input type="text" id="passengerBox" size="3" value="0"><br>
<button type="button" onclick="checkHeight()">Check Height</button>
<div id="outputDiv"></div>
</body>
</html>
```

Desk Check

driver	passenger	message
48	56	

Exclusive Or

It is interesting to consider the English equivalents of each of the logical operators as shown in the following table.

JavaScript Logical Operators

Operator	Name	English Equivalent
!	Not	not
&&	And	and
||	Inclusive Or (Or)	or
^	Exclusive Or (Xor)	either ... or

In English, we often use the word "not" to indicate the absence or opposite of something. For example in the sentence, "This is not good," the word "not" indicates the absence of good or perhaps the opposite of good. This is similar to the logical Not operator. We use the word "and" to indicate a combination of things. For example, "She wore a red hat and a white shirt," meaning that she wore both articles of clothing. This is similar to the logical And operator. We use the word "or" to indicate a choice, such as "You may choose a slice of cake or a slice of pie." This is similar to the logical Inclusive Or operator.

Of the four logical operators taught in this chapter, Exclusive Or is the only one that doesn't have a single English word equivalent. Of the four operators, Exclusive Or is also the least commonly used. It is difficult to find non-trivial, everyday examples of its use. One trivial example is this question and its answer:

> "Where is Jonas?"
> "He is at the library or the soccer field."

In this answer, if we think of the word "or" as Inclusive Or, then according to the answer, it would be possible for Jonas to be at both the library and the soccer field at the same time. Of course, the person answering the question certainly did not mean to imply that Jonas might be at both the library and the soccer field at the same time. Rather the person answering meant, Jonas is at *either* the library *or* the soccer field.

Examples of logical Exclusive Or are rare in programs. Here is a small programming example from a program that includes buttons in its user interface. This code is used to enable or disable a button.

```
if (isEnabled == false && command == 'enable') {
    // enable button
}
else if (isEnabled == true && command == 'disable') {
    // disable button
}
```

Notice that the above code example does nothing if a button is already enabled and the command is to enable the button. It also does nothing if the button is already disabled and the command is to disable the button. It does something only if the state of the button is different from the command. Because of this, it is possible to rewrite the code to use logical Exclusive Or.

```
if (isEnabled == true ^ command == 'enable') {
    // toggle button
}
```

Examples of logical Exclusive Or in programs are so rare that some programming languages, such as C++, don't include a logical Exclusive Or operator. In such languages, a programmer can use the Not Equal operator (!=) in place of logical Exclusive Or. In C++, the previous example could be written like this.

```
if ((isEnabled == true) != (command == 'enable')) {
    // toggle button
}
```

Logical Equivalences

A logical expression can be written in many different ways that resolve to the same result. Two different logical expressions that resolve to the same result are said to be **equivalent**, which is shown with a double ended arrow (⟺). Two such expressions are not the same and are not equal but are equivalent. Here is a list of logical expressions with an equivalent expression for each. Within this list of logical equivalences, the variables *a*, *b*, and *c* each represent some condition. For example, the variable *a* may represent "if (gpa > 3.5)" and *b* may represent "if (credits >= 32)".

1. double negation: Not Not a ⟺ a
2. commutative laws:
    a. a Or b ⟺ b Or a
    b. a And b ⟺ b And a
3. associative laws
    a. (a Or b) Or c ⟺ a Or (b Or c)
    b. (a And b) And c ⟺ a And (b And c)
4. distributive laws
    a. a Or (b And c) ⟺ (a Or b) And (a Or c)
    b. a And (b Or c) ⟺ (a And b) Or (a And c)
5. idempotent laws
    a. a Or a ⟺ a
    b. a And a ⟺ a
6. identity laws
    a. a Or false ⟺ a
    b. a Or true ⟺ true
    c. a And false ⟺ false
    d. a And true ⟺ a
7. negation laws
    a. a Or Not a ⟺ true
    b. a And Not a ⟺ false

Programming Fundamentals in JavaScript

8. absorption laws
   a. a Or (a And b) ⇔ a
   b. a And (a Or b) ⇔ a
9. De Morgan's laws
   a. Not (a Or b) ⇔ Not a And Not b
   b. Not (a And b) ⇔ Not a Or Not b
   c. a Or b ⇔ Not (Not a And Not b)
   d. a And b ⇔ Not (Not a Or Not b)

You may have seen a similar list when you were learning arithmetic. For example, the following list contains three laws for negation, addition, and multiplication.

1. double negation: - - a ⇔ a
2. commutative laws:
   a. a + b ⇔ b + a
   b. a * b ⇔ b * a
3. associative laws:
   a. (a + b) + c ⇔ a + (b + c)
   b. (a * b) * c ⇔ a * (b * c)

It is unnecessary to memorize these types of lists. However, examining the logical equivalences will help you to solidify your knowledge of logic. Consider the double negation equivalence:

Not Not a ⇔ a

If we translate Not into its corresponding JavaScript symbol (!), we can write:

! ! a ⇔ a

If we substitute a specific condition such as "age > 8" in place of *a*, then we have:

```
if (! (! (age > 8)))   ⇔   if (age > 8)
```

It should make sense to you that "if (! (! (age > 8)))" is equivalent to "if (age > 8)" because Not (!) switches true to false and false to true, and switching a boolean value twice results in the original value.

Consider the first logical commutative law:

a Or b ⇔ b Or a

Let's substitute "(age > 8)" in place of *a* and "(gender == "M")" in place of *b* and rewrite the law as JavaScript code:

```
if (age > 8 || gender == "M")   ⇔   if (gender == "M" || age > 8)
```

In other words, the first logical commutative law tells us that it doesn't matter if we write

```
if (age > 8 || gender == "M")
```

or

```
if (gender == "M" || age > 8)
```

in our program. Both if statements will give us the same result.

Using De Morgan's Law

Your school desires to help average students improve their grades. The dean of your college has asked you to write a program to print a list of students who are *not* on the dean's list for academic excellence. You know that the requirements to be on the dean's list are to have a GPA greater than 3.5 and have completed at least 32 credits. However, your program is supposed to print a list of all the students who are *not* on the dean's list. How can you write an if statement to decide to print a student's name or not? Start with the dean's list criteria:

```
if (gpa > 3.5 && credits >= 32) {
    document.getElementById('outputDiv').innerHTML =
            name + " is on the dean's list.";
}
```

The above code will print a student's name if the student qualifies for the dean's list. However, your program is supposed to print a list of all the students who are not on the dean's list. So, you simply add a Not (!) to negate or reverse the sense of the boolean expression.

```
if (!(gpa > 3.5 && credits >= 32)) {
    document.getElementById('outputDiv').innerHTML =
            name + ' is on the average list.';
}
```

This new if statement works but is a bit sloppy and not very understandable. You realize that the condition looks like the left half of De Morgan's law part b. So, you decide to rewrite the condition. From De Morgan's law we see that Not (a And b) ⇔ Not a Or Not b, so you can rewrite the previous expression as:

```
if (!(gpa > 3.5) || !(credits >= 32)) {
    document.getElementById('outputDiv').innerHTML =
            name + ' is on the average list.';
}
```

Which can be simplified as:

```
if (gpa <= 3.5 || credits < 32) {
    document.getElementById('outputDiv').innerHTML =
            name + ' is on the average list.';
}
```

This final expression is simple to understand and correctly determines if a student is not on the dean's list.

Advanced Word Search

The logical operators &&, ||, and ! can be used when searching for documents on your computer or on the internet. At google and other search engines, this is often known as advanced search and can be very powerful. Learning to use advanced search will make you more efficient when searching for information and will help you better understand boolean logic.

Example 5

Imagine you are trying to find the web page for every Madison County in the United States except Idaho. To find these web pages, you might think of a boolean logic query such as

```
madison && (county || parish) && !idaho
```

meaning look for all documents that include "Madison" and either "County" or "Parish" (because Louisiana has parishes and not counties) but exclude "Idaho". Using the advanced search form at google, we enter madison, county, parish, and idaho in the correct text boxes as shown in Figure 7-1. Notice in the top most text box of Figure 7-1 that the google advanced search form wrote the search query as I entered the words in the other text boxes. From this, we learn that the google advanced query that corresponds to our boolean logic query is

```
madison county OR parish -idaho
```

The google advanced query doesn't require the And (&&) operator or parentheses. If there is no operator between two words, the google search engine assumes the user meant And. Also, the Or operator has a higher precedence than And, so the parentheses are unnecessary in our particular search.

Figure 7-1: The advanced search page at google.

Example 6

Look on the internet to find a small flatbed trailer to purchase in southeast Idaho. craigslist.org is a good place to look for advertisements selling a trailer. Unfortunately, at craigslist there isn't a single category for trailers. Instead, trailers are listed in the bikes, cars+trucks, farm+garden, motorcycles, and rvs categories. It would take far too long to look in all of these categories. So, use google to do the search and restrict the search to craigslist and east Idaho.

1. At craigslist.org, click "idaho" then "east idaho" and notice the domain for eastern Idaho is eastidaho.craigslist.org.
2. At google use advanced search with the following criteria:

```
flatbed trailer -gooseneck site:eastidaho.craigslist.org
```

which will cause google to search for advertisements posted to craigslist to sell a flatbed, non-gooseneck trailer in east Idaho. To understand better this google search criteria, notice that it can be rewritten to use JavaScript boolean logic operators like this:

```
flatbed && trailer && !gooseneck && site==eastidaho.craigslist.org
```

Truth Tables

Truth tables can help us to analyze logic, to write simpler boolean expressions, and to prove certain propositions about boolean expressions. We create a truth table by considering two or more conditions. These can be any conditions, for example "if (gpa > 3.5)" or "if (balance > 100)". We label these conditions a, b, c, etc. Then in the columns beneath the named conditions (a, b, c, etc.), we write all possible combinations of false and true. For example, if a boolean expression includes two conditions, a and b, then

1. both the conditions may be false;
2. a may be false and b true;
3. b may be false and a true; or
4. both may be true.

These four combinations are shown in the truth tables below. After writing all possible combinations of true and false in the left columns of the table, we write the logic that we want to evaluate as the heading in the right side of the table. Then we evaluate that logic using the true and false values given in the left columns.

Example 7

Given any two conditions *a* and *b*, show Not a, Not b, a And b, a Or b, a Xor b

1	*2*	*3*	*4*	*5*	*6*	*7*
a	**b**	**!a**	**!b**	**a && b**	**a || b**	**a ^ b**
False	False	True	True	False	False	False
False	True	True	False	False	True	True
True	False	False	True	False	True	True
True	True	False	False	True	True	False

To solve this problem:

1. We draw a truth table with a row for the headings and four rows for boolean values.
2. In columns *1* and *2*, we write the headings **a** and **b** and all possible combinations of true and false.
3. In the heading row for columns *3 – 7*, we translate the logical operators into JavaScript operators.
4. In column *3*, we write the results for !a. Notice that the values in column *3* are the opposite of the values in column *1*.
5. In column *4*, we write the results for !b. Notice that the values in column *4* are the opposite of the values in column *2*.
6. We write the result of (a && b) in column *5*.
7. We write the result of (a || b) in column *6*.
8. We write the result of (a ^ b) in column *7*.

Example 8

Given any two conditions *a* and *b*, show the result of (a Or b) And Not a

1	*2*	*3*	*5*	*4*
a	**b**	**(a || b)**	**&&**	**!a**
False	False	False	False	True
False	True	True	True	True
True	False	True	False	False
True	True	True	False	False

To solve this problem:

1. We draw a truth table with a row for the headings and four rows for boolean values.
2. In columns *1* and *2*, we write the headings **a** and **b** and all possible combinations of true and false.
3. In the heading row for columns *3, 4,* and *5*, we translate the logical expression: (a Or b) And Not a into JavaScript operators: (a || b) && !a
4. We write the result of (a || b) in column *3*. We write column *3* before columns *4* and *5* because a || b is inside parentheses.
5. We write the result of !a in column *4*. We write column *4* before column *5* because Not is a unary operator and has a higher precedence than And.

6. Finally, in column *5* we combine the results of columns *3* and *4* using &&. Column *5* is the result of (a Or b) And Not a.

Example 9

Given any two conditions *a* and *b*, prove that Not (a Or b) ⇔ Not a And Not b

1	*2*	*4*	*3*		*5*	*7*	*6*
a	**b**	**!**	**(a || b)**	⇔	**!a**	**&&**	**!b**
False	False	True	False		True	True	True
False	True	False	True		True	False	False
True	False	False	True		False	False	True
True	True	False	True		False	False	False

To solve this problem:

1. We draw a truth table with a row for the headings and four rows for boolean values.
2. In columns *1* and *2*, we write the headings **a** and **b** and all possible combinations of true and false.
3. In the heading row for columns *3* and *4*, we translate the logical expression: Not (a Or b) into JavaScript operators: !(a || b).
4. In the heading row columns *5*, *6*, and *7*, we translate the logical expression: Not a And Not b into JavaScript operators: !a && !b
5. We write the result of (a || b) in column *3*. We write column *3* before column *4* because a || b is inside parentheses.
6. We write the result of !(a || b) in column *4* which finishes all the logic on the left side of the equivalency arrow (⇔).
7. We write the result of !a in column *5*.
8. We write the result of !b in column *6*.
9. In column *7*, we combine columns *5* and *6* using && which finishes all the logic on the left side of the equivalency arrow (⇔).
10. Finally, we compare the results in columns *4* and *7* and because they are the same, we have proven that Not (a Or b) ⇔ Not a And Not b. In other words, we computed Not (a Or b) for all possible combinations of true and false, and we computed Not a And Not b for all possible combinations of true and false, and we found in all cases that the results were the same. Because Not (a Or b) always gives the same results as Not a And Not b, the two logical expressions are equivalent.

Example 10

Given any two conditions *a* and *b*, show the result of (a And b) Xor Not (a Or b)

1	2	3	6	5	4
a	**b**	**(a && b)**	**^**	**!**	**(a || b)**
False	False	False	True	True	False
False	True	False	False	False	True
True	False	False	False	False	True
True	True	True	True	False	True

To solve this problem:

1. We draw a truth table with a row for the headings and four rows for boolean values.
2. In columns *1* and *2*, we write the headings **a** and **b** and all possible combinations of true and false.
3. In the heading row for columns *3 – 4*, we translate the logical expression: (a And b) Xor Not (a Or b) into JavaScript operators: (a && b) ^ !(a || b)
4. We write the result of (a && b) in column *3*. We write column *3* before columns *6* and *5* because a && b is inside parentheses.
5. We write the result of (a || b) in column *4*. We write column *4* before columns *6* and *5* because a || b is inside parentheses.
6. We write the result of !(a || b) in column *5*.
7. Finally, in column *6*, we combine the results in columns *3* and *5* using ^. In column *6* is the result of (a && b) ^ !(a || b)

If we compare the results in column 6 with the result of a ^ b in example 5, we can see that the result in column *6* is the inverse or opposite of a ^ b. In other words, the long boolean expression given in example 8: (a And b) Xor Not (a Or b) is equivalent to this shorter boolean expression: Not (a Xor b), and we can prove that with a truth table:

1	2	3	6	5	4		8	7
a	**b**	**(a && b)**	**^**	**!**	**(a || b)**	**⇔**	**!**	**(a ^ b)**
False	False	False	True	True	False		True	False
False	True	False	False	False	True		False	True
True	False	False	False	False	True		False	True
True	True	True	True	False	True		True	False

Notice that the results in columns *6* and *8* are the same, so we have proven that (a And b) Xor Not (a Or b) is equivalent to Not (a Xor b). What practical application does this have for a program? Assume that *a* in the above truth table stands for "if (temp < 32)" and that *b* stands for "if (humidity > 0.5)". If we found this if statement in code:

```
if ((temp < 32 && humidity > 0.5) ^ !(temp < 32 || humidity > 0.5)) {
```

we could replace it with this if statement:

```
if ( !(temp < 32 ^ humidity > 0.5) ) {
```

which is equivalent (gives the same result) but is much shorter.

Example 11

Given any three conditions *a*, *b*, and *c*, prove (a Or b) Or c ⟺ a Or (b Or c)

1	*2*	*3*	*4*	*5*		*7*	*6*
a	**b**	**c**	**(a || b)**	**|| c**	⟺	**a ||**	**(b || c)**
False	False	False	False	False		False	False
False	False	True	False	True		True	True
False	True	False	True	True		True	True
False	True	True	True	True		True	True
True	False	False	True	True		True	False
True	False	True	True	True		True	True
True	True	False	True	True		True	True
True	True	True	True	True		True	True

To solve this problem:

1. We draw a truth table with a row for the headings and eight rows for boolean values.
2. In columns *1*, *2*, and *3*, we write the headings **a**, **b**, and **c** and all possible combinations of true and false.
3. In column *4*, we write the result of (a || b).
4. In column *5*, we write the result of combining column *4* with c.
5. In column *6*, we write the result of (b || c).
6. In column *7*, we write the result of combining column *6* with a.
7. Column *5* contains the result of (a || b) || c. Column *7* contains the result of a || (b || c). We see the results in columns *5* and *7* are the same. Therefore, the two logical expressions are equivalent.

Programming Fundamentals in JavaScript

Common Mistakes

Forgetting the left-hand side of a second comparison

Incorrect
```
if (y == 6 || 7) {
}
```

Correct
```
if (y == 6 || y == 7) {
}
```

```
if (y == (6 || 7)) {
}
```

```
if (y == 6, 7) {
}
```

```
if (y == (6, 7)) {
}
```

Forgetting &&

Incorrect
```
if (10 < x < 20) {
}
```

Correct
```
if (10 < x && x < 20) {
}
```

Mixing up the logical operators

Incorrect
```
// This will always be
// true. Think about it.
if (x > 10 || x < 20) {
}
```

Correct
```
// Almost certainly you
// meant to write this:
if (10 < x && x < 20) {
}
```

```
// This will always be
// false.
if (x == 8 && x == 9) {
}
```

```
// Almost certainly you
// meant to write this:
if (x == 8 || x == 9) {
}
```

Unnecessary Comparisons

Incorrect
```
if (age < 8) {
}
if (age >= 8 && x < 12) {
}
if (age >= 12 && age < 18) {
}
if (age >= 18) {
}

if (age < 8) {
}
else if (age >= 8 && age < 12) {
}
else if (age >= 12 && age < 18) {
}
else if (age >= 18) {
}
```

Correct
```
if (age < 8) {
}
else if (age < 12) {
}
else if (age < 18) {
}
else {
}
```

Chapter Summary

- We can use the logical operators to combine multiple comparisons in the condition of a single if statement.
- The JavaScript logical operators are: Not (!), And (&&), Inclusive Or (||), and Exclusive Or (^).
- Not (!) has a higher precedence than the other logical operators because it is a unary operator.
- The logical operators can also be used in an online search to refine the results of the search. However, the logical And operator might not be explicitly written in the search query but may be implied by a space character.
- We can use logical equivalences to rewrite logical expressions in a way that is shorter or clearer.
- We can use a truth table to help us discover and prove logical equivalences.
- De Morgan's laws are a group of four logical equivalences that are commonly used when rewriting logical expressions that include the Not logical operator.

Review Questions

1. The following if statement contains a logic error, not a syntax error. Rewrite it so that it is correct. Assume the variable *age* already exists and holds a valid number.
```
if (18 < age < 30) {
```

2. The following if statement contains a logic error, not a syntax error. Rewrite it so that it is correct. Assume the variable *age* already exists and holds a valid number.
```
if (18 < age || age < 30) {
```

3. The following `if` statement contains a logic error, not a syntax error. Rewrite it so that it is correct. Assume the variable *age* already exists and holds a valid number.
   ```
   if (age == 18 && age == 19) {
   ```

4. After the following code executes, what value will the variable *result* hold?
   ```
   var x = 2, y = 6, z = 5;
   var result = (x < 3 && (y < 7 ^ z != 3))
   ```

5. Use DeMorgan's law: Not (a And b) <=> Not a Or Not b
   to rewrite and simplify this if statement
   ```
   if (!(x == 7 && y >= 0)) {
   ```

   Which of the following is correct?
   a. if (x != 7 || y < 0) {
   b. if (x != 7 || y <= 0) {
   c. if (x != 7 && y < 0) {
   d. if (x == 7 && y >= 0) {

6. Use advanced search at google (www.google.com/advanced_search) to find on the internet a recipe for pizza that doesn't include tomato sauce. Besides the dough, what ingredients does the recipe use?

7. Search the online gospel library at scriptures.lds.org to find the verses in the scriptures with the phrase "word of my power". Occasionally the search at scriptures.lds.org doesn't work. If that is the case, you could use the search at lds.org or the advanced search at google (www.google.com/advanced_search) and restrict your search to site:scriptures.lds.org How many **verses** did you find? Who is the "word of my power"?

8. Use a truth table to prove that Not (a Or b) ⇔ Not a And Not b (De Morgan's law)

9. Use a truth table to prove that Not (a Or b) <=/=> (Not a Or b)
   Note that the symbol <=/=> means not equivalent.

10. Write a truth table for this Boolean expression: (a Or b) And Not (a Xor b). Does the result seem familiar? Is it possible to rewrite this boolean expression more simply and get the same result? What is the simplified expression?

11. Write a truth table for this Boolean expression: (a And b) Xor Not (b Or c)

Programming Assignments

1. Write a defining table and a program that asks the user to enter a month name (January, February, etc) and then outputs the number of days in the month. For February, output "28 or 29 days".

2. You work for a retail store that wants to increase sales on Tuesday and Wednesday, which are the store's slowest sales days. Write a defining table and then a program that takes a customer's subtotal as input and if the subtotal is greater than $50 and today is Tuesday or Wednesday, subtracts 10% from the subtotal. Your program should then compute and output the total amount due by adding sales tax of 6% to the subtotal. Within your program, use this JavaScript code that will get the current day of the week from your computer's clock:

    ```
    var dayOfWeek = new Date().getDay();
    ```

    If you use the above code, the variable *dayOfWeek* will hold 0 if today is Sunday, 1 if today is Monday, and so on to 6 if today is Saturday.

3. Write a defining table and then a program that determines if you can sleep in or not. Your program should get all its input from your computer's clock. On all weekdays (Monday through Friday) that are not holidays, your program should output "Get up!" On all other days (weekends and holidays), your program should output "Sleep in." The three holidays that your program must check for are January 1 (New Year's Day), July 4 (U.S. Independence Day), and December 25 (Christmas). You don't need to include other holidays in your program because most other holidays do not occur on a fixed day each year.

    Within your program, use this JavaScript code that will get the current month, current day of the month, and current day of the week from your computer's clock:

    ```
    var now = new Date();
    var month = now.getMonth();
    var dayOfMonth = now.getDate();
    var dayOfWeek = now.getDay();
    ```

    If you use the above code, the variable *month* will hold 0 if the current month is January, 1 if February, and so on to 11 if December. The variable *dayOfMonth* will hold 1 for the first day of the month up to 28, 29, 30, or 31 for the last day of the month. The variable *dayOfWeek* will hold 0 if today is Sunday, 1 if today is Monday, and so on to 6 if today is Saturday.

4. Write defining table and then a program to determine if you and your date will be allowed to eat in a fancy and fashionable restaurant. Your program should read two integers from the keyboard, one that specifies your fashion measure from 1 to 10, inclusive and one that specifies your date's fashion measure from 1 to 10, inclusive. If either of your fashion measures is 2 or less, your program should output "Not a chance". If either of your fashion measures is 8 or greater, your program should output "Welcome". If your fashion measures sum to more than 12 your program should output, "Maybe". Otherwise, your program should output "Unlikely".

5. Write a defining table and then a program that determines what time a child should go to bed. Your program must read a child's age and the season (winter, spring, summer, or fall) from the keyboard and output the child's bedtime according to this table:

Age	Season	Bed Time
5 or younger	summer, fall	8:30 p.m.
5 or younger	winter, spring	8:00 p.m.
6 to 12	summer	9:30 p.m.
6 to 12	winter, spring, fall	8:30 p.m.
13 and older	summer	10:30 p.m.
13 and older	winter, spring, fall	9:30 p.m.

Chapter 8. Repetition

A computer programmer can cause a computer to repeat a series of statements by writing a loop in a computer program. Every loop includes a boolean condition. Each time the computer needs to decide if it should repeat the statements inside a loop, the computer evaluates the loop's boolean condition. If the condition evaluates to true, then the computer repeats the statements inside the loop. If the condition evaluates to false, the computer does not repeat the statements inside the loop but instead continues executing the program starting with the statements after the loop.

Chapter Outcomes

By the end of this chapter, you will:

- Be able to distinguish between pre-test and post-test loops and between counting and sentinel controlled loops.
- Know when to use a pre-test or post-test loop and when to use a counting or sentinel controlled loop.
- Be able to read and write while, for, and do-while loops that cause a computer to repeat a group of statements.
- Know what the keyword break inside a loop causes a computer to do.

Pre-test and Post-test Loops

Loops can be categorized according to where the boolean condition is located. A **pre-test loop** has the condition at the top of the loop. It is known as a pre-test loop because the condition is evaluated *before* (pre) the computer executes the statements inside the loop. A **post-test loop** has the condition at the bottom of the loop. It is called a post-test loop because the condition is evaluated *after* (post) the statements inside the loop are executed.

With a pre-test loop, the statements inside the loop may never be executed. This is because when the computer encounters the loop, the first thing the computer will do is to evaluate the loop's condition. If the condition evaluates to false, then the computer will not execute the statements inside the loop.

With a post-test loop, the statements inside the loop will always be executed at least once because when the computer encounters the loop, it will first execute the statements inside the loop, and then it will evaluate the loop's condition.

Pre-test loops are used much more frequently than post-test loops. In fact all post-test loops can be rewritten as pre-test loops, so post-test loops are not strictly necessary in a programming language, but they are sometimes convenient to use.

Counting and Sentinel Controlled Loops

Loops can also be categorized by what is in their condition. A **counting loop** causes the computer to count from a start value to an end value. A counting loop's condition is a simple check to see if the counting variable has reached the end value. A **sentinel controlled loop** causes the computer to repeat statements until some event occurs or the computer encounters some sentinel value. A sentinel controlled loop's condition checks for the occurrence of that event or that sentinel value.

Repetition Control Structures

JavaScript has four different ways to write a repetition control structure to cause a computer to repeat statements. The four ways are: while, for, for-each, and do-while. The while, for, and for-each loops are pre-test loops. The do-while loop is a post-test loop. The while, for, and do-while loops all have a condition and repeat the statements inside of them while the condition is true. The for-each loop repeats the statements inside the loop once for each attribute in an object (see chapter 11).

while

Use a while loop when:

- You need a simple counting loop; or
- You cannot use a simple counting loop, so you must use a sentinel controlled loop, and the sentinel must be checked before executing the statements inside the loop.

Template

```
while (condition) {
    statements;
}
```

Figure 8-1 shows a while loop and the order in which the computer executes its parts.

Example 1

```
var i = 1;
while (i < 3) {
    // Statements to be repeated go here.
    alert(i);
    i++;
}
```

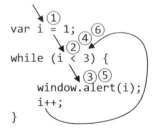

```
var i = 1;
while (i < 3) {
    window.alert(i);
    i++;
}
```

Figure 8-1: A while loop and the order that the computer executes its parts.

Desk Check

i

Programming Fundamentals in JavaScript

for

The for loop is a shortened way of writing a counting while loop. Use a for loop when:

- You need a simple counting loop.

Template

```
for (initialization; condition; update) {
    statements;
}
```

Within the parentheses of a for loop there must always be three statements separated by two semicolons. The three statements are:

1. The initialization statement which is executed only once at the beginning of the loop.
2. The condition that the computer checks to see if it should continue to execute the statements inside the body of the loop. The computer checks this condition after the initialization statement and each time at the beginning of the loop.
3. The update statement that the computer executes each time through the loop as if it were written as the last statement in the body of the loop.

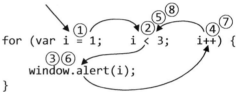

Figure 8-2 shows a for loop and the order in which the computer executes the statements in the parentheses and the body.

Figure 8-2: A for loop and the order that the computer executes its parts.

Example 2

```
for (var i = 1;  i < 3;  i++) {
    // Statements to be repeated go here.
    alert(i);
}
```

Desk Check

Within the parentheses of a for loop there must always be three statements separated by two semicolons. However, you may leave any or all of the statements empty, but you must always include the two semicolons as shown in example 3.

Example 3

```
var i = parseInt(document.getElementById('inputBox').value);
for ( ;  i <= 5;  i++) {
    // Statements to be repeated go here.
    alert(i);
}
```

Desk Check

For Each Loop

The for-each loop is a special case of the for loop. The for-each loop causes the statements inside of it to be repeated once for each attribute in an object (see chapter 11). Use a for-each loop when:

- The statements in the loop must be repeated once for each element in an object.

Template

```
for (variable in object) {
    statements;
}
```

Example 4

```
var text = '';
for (var part in document) {
    // Statements to be repeated go here.
    text += part + ': ' + document[part] + '<br>';
}
document.getElementById('outputDiv').innerHTML = text;
```

do while

The do-while loop is the only post-test loop in JavaScript. The other three loops: while, for, and for-each are pre-test loops.

Use a do-while loop when:

- You can't use a simple counting loop, so you must use a sentinel controlled loop; and
- The statements inside the loop must be executed before checking the sentinel.

Template

```
do {
    statements;
} while (condition);
```

Figure 8-3 shows a do-while loop and the order in which the computer executes its parts. The statements in the body of a post-test loop will always be executed at least once because the test to continue the loop is at the bottom and is evaluated after the statements in the body are executed. The statements in a pre-test loop (while, for, and for-each) may never be executed because the test is at the top of those loops and evaluated before the statements in the body.

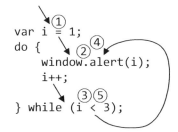

Figure 8-3: A do-while loop and the order that the computer executes its parts.

Here is a do-while loop that asks a user to enter her name and verify that her name is correct. If the user does not enter "yes" when the computer asks if her name is correct, then the computer will repeat the statements in the body of the loop and ask for the user's name again.

Example 5

```
var alias, response;
do {
    // Get the user's name.
    alias = prompt("What is your name?");

    // Ask the user if that is really her name.
    response = prompt("Are you sure " +
        alias + " is your name?");

} while (response != "yes");

// Say hello to the user.
alert("Hello " + alias);
```

Desk Check

alias	response
~~"Sarah"~~	~~"no"~~
"Heidi"	"yes"

Simple Counting Loop

A computer programmer can write a simple counting loop with either a while loop or a for loop. For a simple counting loop, it is up to the programmer to choose the type of loop that makes the most sense to him. However, most experienced programmers will use a for loop to write a simple counting loop. Here are two counting loops that open a popup window three times. Example 6 contains a loop that ascends (counts up), and example 7 contains a loop that descends (counts down).

Example 6

```
var i = 1;
while (i <= 3) {
    alert("leaf");
    i++;
}
```

Desk Check

i

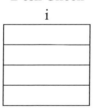

Example 7

```
for (var i = 3;  i >= 1;  i--) {
    alert("caterpillar");
}
```

Desk Check

i

Zero-Based Counting Loop

Experienced computer programmers usually write counting loops to begin at zero (0) rather than one (1). There are likely many reasons programmers start loops at zero; one of them is because array elements (see chapter 10) are indexed starting with zero in C, C++, Java, and JavaScript. Because zero-based counting loops are so common and useful in computer programming, an aspiring programmer must learn to write them. Below are two examples of zero-based counting loops that execute the statements inside the loops exactly 3 times.

Example 8

```
var i = 0;
while (i < 3) {
    alert("stem");
    i++;
}
```

Desk Check

Example 9

```
for (var i = 0;  i < 3;  i++) {
    alert("blossom");
}
```

Desk Check

Skipping Loop

Sometimes we want the computer to count by a number other than one (1). We can easily write a loop that will count by some other number by using the += or the -= operator instead of the ++ or -- operator. Of course, counting in this way will cause the computer to skip some numbers.

Example 10

```
var i = 0;
while (i < 12) {
    alert("aphid");
    i += 4;
}
```

Desk Check

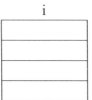

Example 11

```
for (var i = 0;  i < 5;  i += 2) {
    alert("butterfly");
}
```

Desk Check

Programming Fundamentals in JavaScript

Infinite Loop

What does the computer do if a programmer forgets to write the update part of a loop? For example:

```
var i = 0;
while (i < 5) {
    alert('Hello');
}
```

Or this example:

```
for (var i = 0;  i < 5;  ) {
    alert('Hello');
}
```

Notice in both examples that i++ is missing. In other words, after the value of the counting variable *i* is initialized to zero (0), its value is never changed. This means that *i* will start at the value zero, and each time the computer evaluates the boolean condition (i < 5), *i* will be less than 5. In other words, the condition will always evaluate to true, and the computer will keep repeating the statements inside the loop forever or until the user kills the program. This is called an **infinite loop** and is usually, although not always, a mistake. Of course the way to fix both of the above infinite loop examples is to add code to change the value of *i* within the body of the loops, for example:

```
var i = 0;
while (i < 5) {
    alert('Hello');
    i++;
}

for (var i = 0;  i < 5;  i += 2) {
    alert('Hello');
}
```

The reason that an experienced programmer normally uses a for loop to write a simple counting loop is because if she uses a while loop, she may forget to write the update part (i++) which will result in an infinite loop. Instead, if she uses a for loop, she will not forget to write the update part because she will have to write the update part at the same time that she writes the initialization and boolean condition parts.

Compound Interest

Many bank accounts and other investments pay compound interest on the money that is saved in the account. This means each time the bank pays interest, the interest is added to the original money, which is called the principal. Then the next time the bank pays interest, it pays interest on the principal and the previous interest. The balance of such an account and its compound interest can easily be computed using a loop.

Example 12

```
<!DOCTYPE HTML>
<html lang="en-us">
<head>
<meta charset="utf-8">
<title>Compound Interest</title>

<script>
/* Input:
 *      An amount to invest: balance
 *      The annual rate of growth: annualRate
 *      The number of months to invest: numMonths
 * Processing: Use a loop to compute the balance of an account after
 *      a bank has paid interest for numMonths number of months.
 * Output: The balance after numMonths have passed.
 */
function futureValue() {
    var balance = parseFloat(document.getElementById('balance').value);
    var annualRate =parseFloat(document.getElementById('annualRate').value);
    var numMonths = parseInt(document.getElementById('months').value);
    var monthlyRate = annualRate / 12;

    // For each month, compute the interest and add it to the balance.
    for (var month = 1;  month <= numMonths;  month++) {
        // Compute the interest for a month.
        var interest = balance * monthlyRate;

        // Round the interest to pennies.
        interest = Math.round(interest * 100) / 100;

        // Add the interest to the balance.
        balance += interest;
    }

    // Display the resulting balance for the user to see.
    document.getElementById('output').innerHTML =
        "Your balance after " + numMonths + " months will be $" + balance;
}
</script>
</head>

<body>
Balance: <input type="text" id="balance" size="7"><br>
```

```
Annual growth rate: <input type="text" id="annualRate" size="5"><br>
Number of months: <input type="text" id="months" size="3"><br>
<button type="button" onclick="futureValue()">Future Value</button>
<div id="output"></div>
</body>
</html>
```

Desk Check

annualRate	monthlyRate	numMonths	month	interest	balance
0.06		3			100

break

The break keyword causes the computer to end a loop prematurely. It is normally used inside an if statement that is inside a loop. Here is a code example that reads 10 or fewer numbers from a user and computes and outputs the sum of those numbers. The code stops reading numbers from the user after 10 numbers or after the user enters zero (0), whichever comes first.

Example 13

```
// Gets 10 or fewer numbers from the user and adds them together.
function sum10() {
    var sum = 0;
    for (var i = 0;  i < 10;  i++) {
        var n = parseFloat(prompt('Please enter a number'));
        if (n == 0) {
            break;
        }
        sum += n;
    }
    alert(sum);
}
```

Desk Check

i	n	sum
	17	
	−3	
	6	
	0	

Prime Numbers

A prime number is a positive integer that is evenly divisible by only two integers, 1 and itself. The numbers 2, 3, 5, and 7 are prime as are 91, 97, and 101. Prime numbers are very important in computing, for example in hash code algorithms and data encryption. There are many well know algorithms, including the sieve of Eratosthenes, for determining if a number is prime. The following JavaScript code uses a naive and slow algorithm to determine if a number is prime, but it works. The code below increments a divisor from 1 to the candidate number, inclusive and repeatedly divides the candidate by the divisor. Each time the divisor divides the candidate without a remainder, then a factor count is incremented. After the divisor loop is finished, if the factor count is 2 (1 plus the candidate itself), the candidate is prime, otherwise it is not prime.

Example 14

```
<!DOCTYPE HTML>
<html lang="en-us">
<head>
<meta charset="utf-8">
<title>Prime Number</title>

<script>
/* Input: an integer
 * Processing: determine if the given integer is prime or not.
 * Output: __ is prime OR __ is not prime */
function isPrime() {
    var candidate = parseInt(document.getElementById('integerBox').value);

    // Count the number of factors that evenly divide candidate.
    var factorCount = 0;
    for (var divisor = 1;  divisor <= candidate;  divisor++) {
        var remainder = candidate % divisor;
        if (remainder == 0) {
            factorCount++;
        }
    }

    // Determine the output and show it to the user.
    var output;
    if (factorCount == 2) {
        output = candidate + ' is prime';
    }
    else {
        output = candidate + ' is not prime';
    }
    document.getElementById('outputDiv').innerHTML = output;
}
</script>
</head>

<body>
Please enter an integer: <input type="text" id="integerBox"><br>
```

Programming Fundamentals in JavaScript

```
<button type="button" onclick="isPrime()">Is Prime</button>
<div id="outputDiv"></div>
</body>
</html>
```

Desk Check

candidate	divisor	remainder	factorCount	output
8				

The algorithm used by the previous code is naive and slow. What improvements could we make to the code to speed it up?

Example 15 contains a different version of the isPrime code that includes three improvements.

1. The divisor loop begins counting at 2 instead of 1.
2. The divisor loop no longer counts factors, but instead ends as soon as the computer determines the candidate number is not prime.
3. In the case of a prime number, the divisor loop does not count all the way to the candidate number but stops at the square root of the candidate number.

Example 15

```
<!DOCTYPE HTML>
<html lang="en-us">
<head>
<meta charset="utf-8">
<title>Prime Number</title>
<script>
/* Input: an integer
 * Processing: determine if the given integer is prime or not.
 * Output: __ is prime OR __ is not prime */
function isPrime() {
    var candidate = parseInt(document.getElementById('integerBox').value);
    var limit = Math.sqrt(candidate);
    var prime = true;

    // Find the first integer that evenly divides candidate.
    for (var divisor = 2;  divisor <= limit;  divisor++) {
        var remainder = candidate % divisor;
        if (remainder == 0) {
            prime = false;
            break;
        }
    }

    // Determine the output and show it to the user.
    var output;
    if (prime) {
        output = candidate + ' is prime';
    }
    else {
        output = candidate + ' is not prime';
    }
    document.getElementById('outputDiv').innerHTML = output;
}
</script>
</head>
<body>
Please enter an integer: <input type="text" id="integerBox"><br>
<button type="button" onclick="isPrime()">Is Prime</button>
<div id="outputDiv"></div>
</body>
</html>
```

Desk Check

candidate	limit	prime	divisor	remainder	output
8					

Programming Fundamentals in JavaScript

Repetitive Strings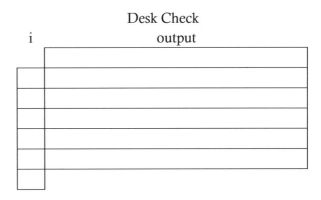

Occasionally we need the computer to produce a string that has a repeating pattern. We can use a loop to cause the computer to build such strings. Consider the string "0, 2, 4, 6, 8, 10" with the simple pattern of counting by twos. Here is code that builds this string and displays it to the user.

Example 16

```
var output = '0';
var i = 2;
while (i <= 10) {
    output += ', ' + i;
    i += 2;
}
document.getElementById('displayDiv').innerHTML = output;
```

Desk Check

i	output

Notice in the above code that the line

```
output += ', ' + i;
```

performs string concatenation and not addition. This is because the starting value for the variable *output* is a string ('0') and because the comma and space (', ') is also a string. The += operator for string concatenation will append new text onto the string each time through the loop so that the value in *output* will grow from '0' to '0, 2' to '0, 2, 4' etc.

Common Mistakes

Writing an infinite loop

Incorrect
```
var i = 0;
while (i < 3) {
    alert("Hello");
}
```

Correct
```
var i = 0;
while (i < 3) {
    alert("Hello");
    i++;
}
// or
for (var i = 0; i < 3; i++) {
    alert("Hello");
}
```

Writing a loop that never repeats

Incorrect
```
for (var i = 0; i > 3; i++) {
}
```

Correct
```
for (var i = 0; i < 3; i++) {
}

// or

for (var i= 0; i != 3; i++) {
}
```

Using commas to separate the parts of a for loop

Incorrect
```
for (var i = 0, i < 5, i++) {
}
```

Correct
```
for (var i = 0; i < 5; i++) {
}
```

Forgetting braces when there is more than one statement inside a loop

Incorrect
```
for (var i = 0; i < n; i++)
    interest = balance * rate;
    balance += interest;
```

Correct
```
for (var i = 0; i < n; i++) {
    interest = balance * rate;
    balance += interest;
}
```

Placing a semicolon at the end of a while loop or for loop

Incorrect
```
var i = 0;
while (i < 3); {
    alert("Hello");
    i++;
}
```

Correct
```
var i = 0;
while (i < 3) {
    alert("Hello");
    i++;
}
```

Incorrect
```
for (var i = 0; i < 3; i++); {
    alert("Hello");
}
```

Correct
```
for (var i = 0; i < 3; i++) {
    alert("Hello");
}
```

Programming Fundamentals in JavaScript

Chapter Summary

- Repetition is the control structure that a programmer uses to cause a computer to repeat a group of statements.
- Loop is the informal term for repetition control structure.
- In a pre-test loop, the loop continuation condition is written at the top of the loop, which causes a computer to check the condition before the computer executes the statements in the loop.
- In a post-test loop, the loop continuation condition is written at the bottom of the loop, which causes a computer to execute the statements in the loop before it checks the condition.
- A counting loop causes a computer to repeat a group of statements until a counting variable reaches a desired number.
- A sentinel controlled loop causes a computer to repeat a group of statements until an event (the sentinel) occurs.
- There are four styles of loops in JavaScript: while, for, for-each, and do-while.
- A while loop is a pre-test loop that is often used as a sentinel controlled loop that causes a computer to repeat the statements inside it while a given condition is true.
- A for loop is a pre-test loop that is used for writing simple counting loops.
- A do-while loop is a post-test loop that is often used as a sentinel controlled loop.

Review Questions

1. Given the following JavaScript code, how many times will the computer display the word "Flowers"?
```
for (var i = 3;  i < 7;  i++) {
    alert("Flowers");
}
```

2. Given the following JavaScript code, how many times will the computer display the word "Apple"?
```
var i = 0;
var limit = 5;
while (i < limit) {
    alert("Apple");
    i += 2;
}
```

3. Given the following JavaScript code, how many times will the computer display the word "Goodbyc"?
```
for (var i = 0;  i > 3;  i++) {
    alert("Goodbye");
}
```

4. Given the following JavaScript code, how many times will the computer display the word "Snow"?
```
var i = 0;
while (i < 3) {
    alert("Snow");
}
```

5. Write a while loop to count from 1 to 10.

6. Write a for loop to count from 1 to 10.

7. Write a loop to count by threes from zero to nine. After the loop is finished, your counting variable should hold the value 9.

8. Write a loop to count backwards from 90 to 81. After the loop is finished, your counting variable should hold the value 81.

9. Write a loop to count forwards by twos from the value in the variable first to the value in the variable last. Assume the variables first and last already exist and hold values.

10. Write a loop to count backwards by twos from the value in the variable last to the value in the variable first. Assume the variables last and first already exist and hold values.

11. Desk check the following code and then write a sentence describing what the code does.
```
function func1() {
    var c = "";
 var a = parseInt(document.getElementById('integerBox').value);
    var b = 100;
        while (b >= 0) {
 c += b + "<br>";
        b -= a;
             }
    document.getElementById('outputDiv').innerHTML = c;
}
```

Desk Check

a	b	c
20		

12. Desk check the following code and then write a sentence describing what the code does. How does this code differ from the code in the previous example? Hint: consider the indentation of the statements in the previous example compared to the indentation of the statements in this example. Also, consider the names of the variables in both examples. Which example is easier to read and desk check?

```javascript
function countDown() {
    var output = "";
    var skip = parseInt(document.getElementById('integerBox').value);
    var i = 100;
    while (i >= 0) {
        output += i + "<br>";
        i -= skip;
    }
    document.getElementById('outputDiv').innerHTML = output;
}
```

Desk Check

skip	i	output
20		

13. Desk check the following code and then write a sentence describing what the code does.

```javascript
function func4() {
        var d = "Please enter an integer.";
var b = 38;
     var c;
  do {
        c = parseInt(prompt(d));
        if (c < b) {
        d = "Too low. Please enter another integer.";
            }
        else if (c > b) {
d = "Too high. Please enter another integer.";
}
        } while (c != b);
    alert(c + " is correct!");
}
```

Desk Check

b	c	d
	25	
	60	
	38	

14. Desk check the following code and then write a sentence describing what the code does. How does this code differ from the code in the previous example? Hint: consider the indentation of the statements in the previous example compared to the indentation of the statements in this example. Also, consider the names of the variables in both examples. Which example is easier to read and desk check?

```javascript
function numberGuessGame() {
    var message =
        "I'm thinking of a number between 1 and 100.\n" +
        "Try to guess it!\n" +
        "Please enter an integer between 1 and 100.";
    var answer = 38;
    var guess;
    do {
        guess = parseInt(prompt(message));
        if (guess < answer) {
            message = guess +
                " is too low. Please enter another integer.";
        }
        else if (guess > answer) {
            message = guess +
                " is too high. Please enter another integer.";
        }
    } while (guess != answer);
    message = guess + " is correct!";
    alert(message);
}
```

Desk Check

answer	guess	message
	25	
	60	
	38	

Programming Assignments

1. Write a defining table and a program that reads an integer *n* from the keyboard and then displays the word "sunshine" *n* times in a div.

2. Write a defining table and a program that reads a phrase and an integer *n* from the keyboard and then displays that phrase *n* times in a div.

3. Write a defining table and a program that asks the user for an integer *n* and then outputs all the integers between 1 and *n*, inclusive.

4. Write a defining table and a program that asks the user for an integer *n* and then outputs the sum of all the odd integers between 1 and *n*, inclusive. For example, if a user entered 10, your program would add $1 + 3 + 5 + 7 + 9$ and output 25. If a user entered 11, your program would add $1 + 3 + 5 + 7 + 9 + 11$ and output 36.

5. Write a defining table and a program to output the five times table from 1 to 12 in this format:

$$5 \times 1 = 5$$
$$5 \times 2 = 10$$
$$\vdots$$
$$5 \times 12 = 60$$

6. Write a defining table and a program to output all powers of 2 from 2^0 up to 2^{31}, inclusive. In other words, your program should output this series: 1, 2, 4, 8, ... 2147483648

7. Write a defining table and a program that outputs the first 25 numbers in this Fibonacci series: 0, 1, 1, 2, 3, 5, 8, ... 46368

8. Rewrite the number guessing game code found in review question 14 so that it counts the number of guesses the user takes to guess correctly the answer.

9. Write a defining table and a program that asks the user for an integer *n* and then outputs the following table.

n	2*n	3*n	n*n	n*n*n
1	2	3	1	1
2	4	6	4	8
3	6	9	9	27
$\vdots$	$\vdots$	$\vdots$	$\vdots$	$\vdots$
n	$2n$	$3n$	n^2	n^3

10. Write a defining table and a program that builds and displays a 12 by 12 multiplication table.

11. Write a defining table and a program that allows a user to enter ten numbers and then computes and outputs the average of those numbers. The user interface for your program should look similar to Figure 8-4. Your program must use a loop to read the ten numbers and compute the sum of those numbers.

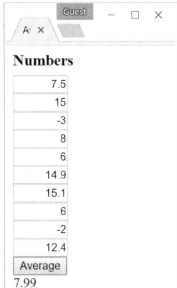

Figure 8-4: An HTML document and JavaScript program that computes the average of ten numbers.

Chapter 9. Functions

Because most useful computer programs are very large, computer programmers divide their programs into parts. A part of a program is called a **module**. In JavaScript the smallest module that performs actions is a **function**, which is sometimes called a **method**. Nearly all statements in a JavaScript program must be written inside a function.

The term function comes from mathematics and is the name of the concept that one value (the **argument** of the function) completely determines another value (the **result** of the function). Consider the function f with one argument x : $f(x) = 2x - 1$. We can substitute any number for the argument x which completely determines the result of the function f. For example, substituting 5 for x produces 9 as the result of the function: $f(5) = 2(5) - 1 = 9$. Functions in a computer program work in a similar way, taking arguments and producing results.

Chapter Outcomes

By the end of this chapter, you will:

- Write functions that accept and use parameters.
- Write code to return a value from a function to its call point.
- Write code to call a function and pass arguments to that function.
- Write code to store the result returned from a function in a variable.
- Distinguish between a parameter and an argument.
- Distinguish between displaying output for the user to see and returning a value to be used by the program.
- Understand local variable scope.

Writing a Function

To write a function in JavaScript, simply type code that matches this template.

Template

```
function functionName(param1, param2, … paramN) {
    statements;
    return value;
}
```

The first line of a function is called the **header** or **signature**, and it includes

1. the keyword `function`
2. the function name
3. the parameter list

The function name must start with a letter, the underscore (_), or the dollar sign ($). The rest of the name must be made of letters, digits (0–9), the underscore, or the dollar sign. A function name cannot include spaces. A function name should be meaningful and should describe curtly what the function does. The **parameter list** contains data stored in variables that the function needs to complete its task.

The statements inside a function are called the **body** of the function. A function may contain as many statements as you wish to write inside of it. However, it is a good idea to limit functions to less than a page (60 lines) long. To **return** a result from a function so that the result can be used somewhere else in your program, simply type the keyword return followed by whatever value you want returned to the calling function.

Example 1

Write the header for a function named drawCircle that takes three parameters: the x and y values for the center of the circle and the radius of the circle, all in pixels.

```
function drawCircle(centerX, centerY, radius)
```

Example 2

Write the header for a function named getDiscountRate, which returns the discount rate applied to a student's car insurance premium. The function requires two parameters: the student's birthday and GPA.

Why does the getDiscountRate function require two parameters? In other words, what rule does the insurance company have that requires getDiscountRate to have two parameters?

Example 3

Write a function (header and body) that computes and returns the average of three numbers.

```
// Computes and returns the average of three numbers.
function average(a, b, c) {
    var sum = a + b + c;
    var avg = sum / 3;
    return avg;
}
```

Example 4

Write a function that takes two parameters and computes and returns the value of this equation: $f(a,r) = a \times (1 + r)$.

Programming Fundamentals in JavaScript

Calling a Function

Calling or **invoking** a function causes the computer to execute the code in that function. If you write a function, but never write a call to that function, then the code in that function will never be executed. To call a function, simply write its name followed by the data, known as **arguments**, which the function will need to perform its task. An argument can be a constant such as 23, a string literal such as 'Idaho', or a variable. If you use variables as arguments in a function call, the names of the arguments do not have to match the names of the parameters. However, the order of the arguments must match the order of the parameters.

Template

```
functionName(arg1, arg2, … argN);
```

Example 5

Write the code to call a function that has this header:

```
function drawCircle(centerX, centerY, radius)
```

```
function run() {
    var x = parseInt(document.getElementById('xInputBox').value);
    var y = parseInt(document.getElementById('yInputBox').value);
    var radius = parseInt(document.getElementById('radiusInputBox').value);
    drawCircle(x, y, radius);
}
```

Example 6

Write code to call a function that has this header:

```
function drawRectangle(x, y, width, height)
```

To call a function *and* assign its result to a variable so the result can be used later, write a line that includes the variable name that will hold the result, the assignment operator (=), the function name, and the arguments to the function.

Template

```
varName = functionName(arg1, arg2, … argN);
```

Example 7

Write code to call the square root function found in the Math object and assign the result returned from it to a variable named *rt*. The square root function has this header:

```
function sqrt(x)
```

```
function testSqrt() {
    var value = 73.1;
    var rt = Math.sqrt(value);
    document.getElementById('outputDiv').innerHTML = rt;
}
```

Example 8

Write code to call a function named computeCaloriesBurned and store the result returned from the function in a variable named *calories*. The function has this header:

```
function computeCaloriesBurned(distance, elevation, weight)
```

Figure 9-1 demonstrates what the computer does when it calls a function. Within a program, a line of code that calls a function is known as a **call point**. As shown in the diagram, the computer first copies the value of each argument at the call point into the corresponding parameter. The computer then executes the code in the body of the called function. Most functions end with a return statement. When the computer executes a return statement in the called function, the return statement causes the computer to do three things.

1. The return statement causes the computer to return a value, which is often a number, to the call point. If the call point includes a variable and the assignment operator (=), the computer will store the returned value in that variable.

2. The return statement causes the computer to terminate the called function or in other words to stop executing the code in the body of the called function.

3. The return statement cause the computer to resume executing code at or after the call point.

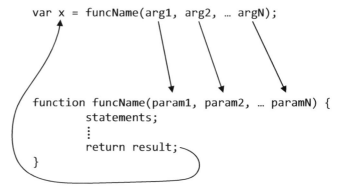

Figure 9-1: Demonstration of a function call, showing how the arguments are assigned to the parameters and showing that when the computer is finished executing the function, the result is returned from the function to the call point.

Programming Fundamentals in JavaScript

Variable Scope

The **scope** of a variable determines how long that variable exists and where it can be used. Within a JavaScript program, there are two categories of scope: local and global. A **local variable** is declared inside a function, exists for as long as its containing function is executing, and can be used within its containing function only. A **global variable** is declared outside all functions, exists for as long as its containing file is loaded in the computer's memory, and can be used within all functions in its containing file. Parameters are local variables because they are declared within a function, specifically within a function's header.

JavaScript Variable Scope

	Local	Global
Where to Declare	Inside a function	Outside all functions
Owner	The function where the variable is declared	The JavaScript program, or stated more accurately, the HTML file that contains the script tag where it is declared
Lifetime	Only as long as its containing function is executing	As long as its containing HTML file is loaded in the computer's memory
Where Usable	Only inside the function where it is declared	In all functions in the JavaScript program

Example 9 contains global and local variables. The variable *attempts* is global because it is declared outside of all functions. Because it is a global variable, the code in the body of all functions may use the variable *attempts*. Within the function sqareArea, there are two local variables named *length* and *area*. Within the function rectangleArea, there are three local variables named *width*, *length*, and *area*. Because local variables are visible only within the function where they are declared, a programmer can declare two variables with the same name as long as he declares them in different functions. In example 9, both of the functions squareArea and rectangleArea contain a local variable named *length* and a local variable named *area*. All four of these variables are entirely separate and do not conflict with each other in any way because the scope of each variable is within the function where it is declared.

Example 9

```
var attempts;

function squareArea(length) {
    var area = length * length;
    return area;
}

function rectangleArea(width, length) {
    var area = width * length;
    return area;
}
```

Advantages of Functions

There are many advantages to writing statements inside a function instead of outside of all functions, including

1. Control of execution – JavaScript statements that are inside an HTML script tag but outside of all functions are executed immediately when a document is read into memory by a browser. Statements that are inside a function are not executed until a function is called which gives the programmer control over when those statements are executed.
2. Code reuse – After a function is written it can be reused again and again by calling it from multiple locations in a program.
3. Less code – Because a programmer can reuse code, he does not have to write as much code.
4. Fewer coding mistakes – writing less code will naturally lead to fewer mistakes because there is simply less code to contain the mistakes.
5. Better organization
6. Easier to read and understand
7. Easier to debug
8. Faster execution – Because a program with well written functions contains less code, that program will very likely load faster and execute faster.
9. Variable name reuse – Because variables declared inside a function are local to that function only, a programmer can reuse variable names in different functions.

Pseudo Random Integer

The following code example shows how to obtain a pseudo random integer that is in the range *min* inclusive to *max* exclusive, in other words in the range [*min*, *max*). Notice that this code calls both the `random` and `floor` functions from the `Math` object.

Example 10

```
var r = min + Math.floor(Math.random() * (max - min));
```

Desk Check

min	max	value returned from Math.random	r
5	11	0.483	

Code Reuse

The most reusable functions are ones that perform only calculations and do not perform user input and output. Chapter 6 contains code to determine if an integer is even or odd. Examples 11 and 12 both contain the example code from chapter six. However, in both examples 11 and 12, the example code is split into two functions: doInputOutput and isEven. The first function, doInputOutput, gets the user input, calls the second function, and displays the result to the user. The first function is certainly useful in this program but is not reusable in another program because it requires a text field with an id of "number" and a div with an id of "output". The second function, isEven, does only one thing: determine if an integer is even or odd. Because the second function does only calculations (it does not get user input nor display results to the user), the second function is reusable in other programs. The second function can be used in any program that needs to determine if an integer is even or odd regardless of where the input comes from, such as a user or a file or anywhere else.

Example 11

```
<!DOCTYPE HTML>
<html lang="en-us">
<head>
<meta charset="utf-8">
<title>Is Even</title>
<script>
/* Input: An integer
 * Processing: Determine if the integer is even or not
 * Output: A message stating if the integer is even or not
 */
function doInputOutput() {
    var number = parseInt(document.getElementById('numberInputBox').value);
    var result = isEven(number);
    document.getElementById('outputDiv').innerHTML =
        number + ' is even: ' + result;
}

// Returns true if value is an even
// integer; otherwise returns false.
function isEven(value) {
    if ((value % 2) == 0) {
        return true;
    }
    else {
        return false;
    }
}
</script>
</head>
<body>
Please enter an integer: <input type="text" id="numberInputBox">
<button type="button" onclick="doInputOutput()">Is Even?</button>
<div id="outputDiv"></div>
</body>
</html>
```

Deck Check

number	result
8	

value	value % 2	return

Because the isEven function returns a boolean value, we can write it without the if statement. Eliminating the if statement makes the function easier to test because the function will contain only one possible path of execution instead of two.

Example 12

```
<!DOCTYPE HTML>
<html lang="en-us">
<head>
<meta charset="utf-8">
<title>Is Even</title>

<script>
/* Input: An integer
 * Processing: Determine if the integer is even or not
 * Output: A message stating if the integer is even or not
 */
function doInputOutput() {
    var number = parseInt(document.getElementById('numberInputBox').value);
    var result = isEven(number);
    document.getElementById('outputDiv').innerHTML =
        number + ' is even: ' + result;
}

// Returns true if value is an even
// integer; otherwise returns false.
function isEven(value) {
    return (value % 2) == 0;
}
</script>
</head>

<body>
Please enter an integer: <input type="text" id="numberInputBox">
<button type="button" onclick="doInputOutput()">Is Even?</button>
<div id="outputDiv"></div>
</body>
</html>
```

Deck Check

number	result
8	

value	value % 2	return

Area of a Triangle

If we know the side lengths of a triangle as shown in Figure 9-2, we can compute the area of that triangle using **Heron's formula** which is

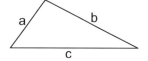

$$area = \sqrt{s(s-a)(s-b)(s-c)}$$

Figure 9-2: An irregular triangle with side lengths *a*, *b*, and *c*.

where *a*, *b*, and *c* are the lengths of the three sides of the triangle and *s* is the semi-perimeter of the triangle defined by

$$s = \frac{a+b+c}{2}$$

Example 13

```
<!DOCTYPE HTML>
<html lang="en-us">
<head>
<meta charset="utf-8">
<title>Triangle Area</title>

<script>
/* Input: No user input
 * Processing: Compute the area of a triangle with side lengths 4, 2, and 5
 * Output: The area of the triangle
 */
function testTriangle() {
    var r = triangleArea(4, 2, 5);
    document.getElementById('outputDiv').innerHTML = r;
}

// Computes and returns the area of a
// triangle with side lengths a, b, and c.
function triangleArea(a, b, c) {
    var s = (a + b + c) / 2;
    var area = Math.sqrt(s * (s-a) * (s-b) * (s-c));
    return area;
}
</script>
</head>
<body>
<button type="button" onclick="testTriangle()">Test</button>
<div id="outputDiv"></div>
</body>
</html>
```

Desk Check

r

a	b	c	s	$(s-a)$	$(s-b)$	$(s-c)$	area

Surface Area of a Pyramid

Imagine designing one of the great pyramids. The stones on the inside of the pyramids are very rough and are essentially just filler. The stones on the outside are finished smooth to reflect sunlight. If you were writing the software to design a pyramid, your software would have to compute the surface area of a pyramid so the builders would know how much finished stone they need to cover the outside of the pyramid.

Figure 9-3 shows a regular pyramid (all four sides are the same size) with edge length e, height h, and base length b. Since it is a regular pyramid, to compute the surface area your software could compute the area of one of the pyramid's triangular faces and multiply that by 4. If the builder of a regular pyramid specified the base length and the height, then your software could use this formula for computing the edge length from the base length and height:

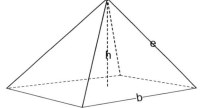

$$e = \sqrt{\frac{b^2}{2} + h^2}$$

Figure 9-3: A regular pyramid with edge length e, height h, and base length b.

and then call the `triangleArea` function shown above to compute the area of one of the triangular faces.

Example 14

```
<!DOCTYPE HTML>
<html lang="en-us">
<head>
<meta charset="utf-8">
<title>Surface Area of a Pyramid</title>

<script>
/* Input: No user input
 * Processing: Compute the surface area of the triangular faces
 *      of a regular pyramid that has base 8 and height 7.
 * Output: The surface area of the pyramid
 */
function testPyramid() {
    var pa = pyramidSurfaceArea(8, 7);
    document.getElementById('outputDiv').innerHTML = pa;
}


// Computes and returns the surface area of the
// four triangular faces of a regular pyramid
// with the specified base length and height.
function pyramidSurfaceArea(base, height) {
    var edge = Math.sqrt(base*base/2 + height*height);
    var triArea = triangleArea(base, edge, edge);
    var pyramidArea = 4 * triArea;
    return pyramidArea;
}


// Computes and returns the area of a
// triangle with side lengths a, b, and c.
function triangleArea(a, b, c) {
    var s = (a + b + c) / 2;
    var area = Math.sqrt(s * (s-a) * (s-b) * (s-c));
    return area;
}
</script>
</head>

<body>
<button type="button" onclick="testPyramid()">Test</button>
<div id="outputDiv"></div>
</body>
</html>
```

Desk Check

pa

base	height	edge	triArea	pyramidArea

a	b	c	s	$(s-a)$	$(s-b)$	$(s-c)$	area

How Long to Invest

A common question when saving and investing money is, "How long will I need to invest a certain amount of money in order for that money to grow to a certain larger amount of money?" For example, how many months will I need to invest $100 at 6% fixed annual growth rate compounded monthly in order for my investment to grow to $103?

Example 15

```
<!DOCTYPE HTML>
<html lang="en-us">
<head>
<meta charset="utf-8">
<title>How Long to Invest</title>
<script>
/* Input: No user input
 * Processing: Determine the number of months required to grow an initial
 *   investment of $100 to at least $103 if it grows at an annual rate of 6%.
 * Output: The number of months. */
function testInvest() {
    var m = determineMonths(100, 0.06, 103);
    document.getElementById('outputDiv').innerHTML = m;
}


// Computes and returns the number of months needed for principal
// invested at a constant annual rate to grow to a target amount.
function determineMonths(principal, annualRate, target) {
    var monthlyRate = annualRate / 12;
    var balance = principal;
    var month = 0;

    // Repeat while the balance of the investment is less than the target.
    while (balance < target) {
        var interest = Math.round(balance * monthlyRate * 100) / 100;
        balance += interest;
        month++;
    }
    return month;
}
</script>
</head>
```

Desk Check

m

principal	annualRate	interest	balance	month

target	monthlyRate


```
<body>
<button type="button" onclick="testInvest()">Test</button>
<div id="outputDiv"></div>
</body>
</html>
```

Programming Fundamentals in JavaScript

Greatest Common Divisor

The greatest common divisor (**gcd**) of two non-zero integers is the largest positive integer that divides both numbers without a remainder. An efficient algorithm to compute the gcd was discovered by Euclid and works like this. Given two integers, 102 and 18,

1. divide 102 by 18 to get a quotient of 5 and a remainder of 12,
2. divide 18 by 12 to get a quotient of 1 and a remainder of 6,
3. divide 12 by 6 to get a quotient of 2 and a remainder of 0
4. the remainder 0 means the greatest common divisor of 102 and 18 is 6.

Euclid's algorithm is written in the next example inside a JavaScript function that has this header: `function gcd(a, b)`. Notice from its header that the gcd function requires two values as parameters. To call this function a programmer must write the name of the function, `gcd`, followed by an argument list with two arguments to match the two parameters, as shown in the `testGCD` function below.

Example 16

```
<!DOCTYPE HTML>
<html lang="en-us">
<head>
<meta charset="utf-8">
<title>Greatest Common Divisor</title>

<script>
/* Input: No user input
 * Processing: Determine the greatest common divisor of -24 and 472
 * Output: The greatest common divisor
 */
function testGCD() {
    var x = -24;
    var y = 472;
    var divisor = gcd(x, y);
    document.getElementById('outputDiv').innerHTML = divisor;
}

// Finds and returns the greatest common
// divisor of two integers a and b.
function gcd(a, b) {
    // Ensure a and b are not negative.
    a = Math.abs(a);
    b = Math.abs(b);

    // Ensure a is greater than or equal to b.
    if (a < b) {
        var swap = a;
        a = b;
        b = swap;
    }

    // Repeat until the computer finds
    // the greatest common divisor.
    do {
        var r = a % b;
        a = b;
        b = r;
    } while (b != 0);

    return a;
}
</script>
</head>

<body>
<button type="button" onclick="testGCD()">Test</button>
<div id="outputDiv"></div>
</body>
</html>
```

Desk Check

x	y	divisor

r	a	b	swap	return value

Programming Fundamentals in JavaScript

Common Mistakes

Putting a space in a function's name

Incorrect
```
function check Answer() {
}
```

Correct
```
function checkAnswer() {
}
```

Forgetting the opening or closing curly brace

Incorrect
```
function sum(x, y, z) {
    var s = x + y + z;
    return s;
```

Correct
```
function sum(x, y, z) {
    var s = x + y + z;
    return s;
}
```

Re-declaring or re-assigning parameters

Incorrect

```
function getDiscountRate(birthday, gpa) {
    // Wrong! Don't re-declare nor assign parameters.
    var birthday = new Date("3/17/1995");
    var gpa = prompt("What is your GPA?");

    var birthYear = birthday.getFullYear();
    var currYear = new Date().getFullYear();
    var age = currYear - birthYear;
    var rate;
    ...
    return rate;
}
```

Correct

```
function getDiscountRate(birthday, gpa) {
    var birthYear = birthday.getFullYear();
    var currYear = new Date().getFullYear();
    var age = currYear - birthYear;
    var rate;
    ...
    return rate;
}
```

Confusing the concepts of return and output

Return means to return a value to the call point of a function. This is entirely internal to a program, and the user will not see anything because of a return statement. To return a result from a JavaScript function, use the keyword `return`.

Output means to show a value to the user. In JavaScript output is done by calling `alert`, `document.write`, or assigning a value to the `innerHTML` attribute of a div (`document.getElementById('resultDiv').innerHTML = x;`).

Chapter Summary

- A module is a part of a program. The term module can refer to a very large part of a program, including many files and functions, or it can refer to a small part of a program such as a single function.
- A function is the smallest part of a program that performs actions and is sometimes called a method. A well written function is a reusable part of a program that performs one task such as calculating the average of a list of numbers or the area of a triangle.
- A function has a header and a body. The header is also known as the signature.
- The header of a function includes the function's parameters. Each parameter is a variable.
- A call point of a function is a line of code in a program where that function is called or invoked. The values for a function's parameters come from a call point of that function.
- The body of a function includes all the statements to perform a single task such as a calculation. The body normally ends with a return statement to return a calculated value to the call point.
- A return statement causes a computer to stop executing the current function, to return a value to the call point of the current function, and to resume executing the code at or after the call point.
- To call a function, write the function's name followed by the arguments that the function will need to perform its task.
- An argument is the value or variable that is passed from the call point into a function.
- To store the value returned from a function write a variable name and the assignment operator (=) at the call point of the function.

Review Questions

1. Consider these three terms: function, module, and program. Order them from largest (contains the most) to smallest (contains the least).

2. What is the JavaScript keyword that begins a function header?

3. Write the header for a function named `computeFutureValue`, which takes as parameters three numbers named `principal`, `annualRate`, and `years`.

4. Write the header for a function named `coneVolume`, which takes as parameters a radius and a height.

5. Within a function header, for example:
   ```
   function gcd(a, b) {
   ```
   the variables that appear within parentheses are called what?

6. Within a function call, for example:
   ```
   var g = gcd(142, y);
   ```
   the text that appears within parentheses is called what?

7. Given this function header:
   ```
   function compute(x, y, z) {
   ```

   and this code to call that function:
   ```
   var x = 7;
   var result = compute(3, 2, x);
   ```

   Within the function compute, what value will be stored in the parameter x?

8. Assume that a function with this header:
   ```
   function addOrder(name, amount)
   ```
   already exists. Write a single line of JavaScript code to call that function.

9. Assume that a function with this header:
   ```
   function isPrime(value)
   ```
   already exists. Write a single line of JavaScript code to call that function and assign the result returned from that function to a variable named *p*.

10. Within a function, what does the keyword return do? (Mark all that apply)
    a. cause the computer to stop executing the current function
    b. return a value to the call point
    c. display a value for a user to see
    d. cause the computer to resume executing code after the call point

Programming Assignments

1. Rewrite the number guessing game code found in review question 14 of chapter 8 so that it
   a. is inside a function with this header: `function numberGuessGame()` which is called when a user clicks a Play button
   b. chooses a different pseudo random number between 1 and 100 each time it runs
   c. counts the number of guesses the user takes to correctly guess the answer

2. Create an HTML document, which contains a text field, a button, and a div. Label the first text field "Fahrenheit" and put the text "Celsius" on the button. Write two functions with these headers:

   ```
   function doInputOutput()
   function fahrToCels(fahr)
   ```

   The first function (doInputOutput) must be called from the onclick attribute of the button and must do the following:
   a. get a temperature in Fahrenheit from the text field
   b. call the second function (fahrToCels)
   c. store the value returned by fahrToCels in a variable

d.   output the value returned by `fahrToCels` to the div for the user to see

The second function (`fahrToCels`) must
    a.   take a temperature in Fahrenheit as a parameter
    b.   calculate the corresponding Celsius temperature
    c.   return the Celsius temperature

In other words, the second function (`fahrToCels`) must not gather any input from a user and must not output anything for a user to see. Instead, it must calculate and return the result, which makes this second function very reusable in other projects.

3.   Create an HTML document, which contains two text fields, a button, and a div. Label the first text field "Temperature", label the second "Wind Speed", and put the text "Wind Chill" on the button. Write two functions with these headers:

```
function doInputOutput()
function windChill(tempF, speed)
```

The first function (`doInputOutput`) must be called from the `onclick` attribute of the button and must do the following:
    a.   get a temperature from the first text field
    b.   get a wind speed from the second text field
    c.   call the second function (`windChill`)
    d.   store the value returned by `windChill` in a variable
    e.   output the value returned by `windChill` to the div for the user to see

The second function (`windChill`) must
    a.   take a temperature in Fahrenheit as a parameter
    b.   take a wind speed in miles per hour as a parameter
    c.   calculate the wind chill factor as a temperature in Fahrenheit
    d.   return the wind chill factor in Fahrenheit

In other words, the second function (`windChill`) must not gather any input from a user and must not output anything for a user to see. Instead, it must calculate and return the result, which makes this second function very reusable in other projects.

The formula for computing the wind chill factor is

$$f = 35.74 + 0.6215\, t - 35.75\, s^{0.16} + 0.4275\, t\, s^{0.16}$$

where f is the wind chill factor in Fahrenheit, t is the air temperature in Fahrenheit, and s is the wind speed in miles per hour at five feet above the ground. Use your function in an HTML and JavaScript program that includes two text fields to input the air temperature and wind speed and a div to output the wind chill factor.

4. Create an HTML document, which contains two text fields, a button, and a div. Label the first text field "Temperature", label the second "Relative Humidity", and put the text "Heat Index" on the button. Write two functions with these headers:

```
function doInputOutput()
function heatIndex(tempF, humid)
```

The first function (doInputOutput) must be called from the onclick attribute of the button and must do the following:

    a.   get a temperature from the first text field
    b.   get a relative humidity from the second text field
    c.   call the second function (heatIndex)
    d.   store the value returned by heatIndex in a variable
    e.   output the value returned by heatIndex to the div for the user to see

The second function (heatIndex) must

    a.   take a temperature in Fahrenheit as a parameter
    b.   take a relative humidity between 0% and 100% as a parameter
    c.   calculate the heat index as a temperature in Fahrenheit
    d.   return the heat index in Fahrenheit

In other words, the second function (heatIndex) must not gather any input from a user and must not output anything for a user to see. Instead, it must calculate and return the result, which makes this second function very reusable in other projects.

The formula for computing the heat index is

$$i = -42.379 + 2.04901523\, t + 10.1433127\, r - 0.22475541\, t\, r - 0.00683783\, t^2$$
$$- 0.05481717\, r^2 + 0.00122874\, t^2\, r + 0.00085282\, t\, r^2$$
$$- 0.00000199\, t^2 r^2$$

where i is the heat index in Fahrenheit, t is the air temperature in Fahrenheit, and r is the relative humidity.

5. Figure 9-4 shows a triangular prism. The volume of a triangular prism can be calculated by multiplying the area of the triangular face by the length of the prism. In other words

$$volume = triangleArea * length$$

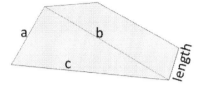

Figure 9-4: a triangular prism

Write a program that calculates the volume of a triangular prism. Your program must allow the user to enter the three side lengths of the triangular face and the length of the prism. Your program must include these three functions:

```
function doInputOutput()
function prismVolume(a, b, c, length)
function triangleArea(a, b, c)
```

The first function (doInputOutput)
  a. takes no parameters
  b. is called from the onclick attribute
  c. gets four numbers from the user
  d. calls the prismVolume function
  e. displays the result to the user

The second function (prismVolume)
  a. takes four parameters
  b. calls the triangleArea function
  c. computes the volume of a prism
  d. returns the volume

The third function (triangleArea)
  a. takes three parameters
  b. computes the area of a triangle
  c. returns the area

Hint: use the triangleArea function that is written in this chapter.

6. Figure 9-5 shows a very basic house. Notice that the roof space of the house is a triangular prism and the living space of the house is a rectangular prism. Write a program that calculates the total volume of the house, including the volume of the roof space. Your program must allow the user to enter the *width*, *depth*, *height*, and *sweep* as shown in Figure 9-5. Here are some useful formulas:

$$houseVolume = livingVolume + roofVolume$$
$$livingVolume = width * depth * height$$
$$roofVolume = triangleArea * width$$
$$triangleArea = \sqrt{s(s-a)(s-b)(s-c)}$$
$$s = \frac{a+b+c}{2}$$

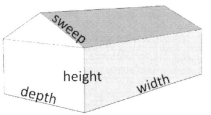

Figure 9-5: a basic house

Your program must include these five functions:

```
function doInputOutput()
function houseVolume(width, depth, height, sweep)
function livingVolume(width, depth, height)
function roofVolume(width, depth, sweep)
function triangleArea(a, b, c)
```

The first function (doInputOutput)
   a.   takes no parameters
   b.   is called from the onclick attribute
   c.   gets four numbers from the user
   d.   calls the houseVolume function
   e.   displays the house volume to the user

The second function (houseVolume)
   a.   takes four parameters
   b.   calls the livingVolume function
   c.   calls the roofVolume function
   d.   computes the house volume by adding the living volume and the roof volume
   e.   returns the house volume

The third function (livingVolume)
   a.   takes three parameters
   b.   computes and returns the volume of the living space

The fourth function (roofVolume)
   a.   takes three parameters
   b.   calls the triangleArea function
   c.   computes and returns the volume of the roof

The fifth function (triangleArea)
   a.   takes three parameters
   b.   computes and returns the area of a triangle
Hint: use the use the triangleArea function that is written in this chapter.

7. Create an HTML document that looks similar to Figure 9-6. Write two functions with these headers:

```
function doFV()
function computeFutureValue(principal, annualRate, years,periodsPerYear)
```

The first function (doFV)
  a. takes no parameters
  b. is called from the `onclick` attribute
  c. gets input from the user
  d. calls the `computeFutureValue` function
  e. displays the result to the user

The second function (`computeFutureValue`) computes and returns the future value of an investment. The formula for computing the future value of an investment is

$$f = a(1 + r)^n$$

where f is the future value, a is the

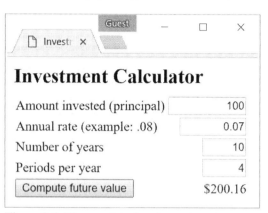

Figure 9-6: The user interface for an investment calculator.

investment amount, r is the growth rate **per period**, and n is the total number of periods **throughout the life of the investment**.

8. Create an HTML document that looks similar to Figure 9-7. Write four functions with these headers:

```
function doPayment()
function doBalance()
function computePayment(principal, annualRate, years, periodsPerYear)
function computeBalance(principal, annualRate, years, periodsPerYear,
        numberOfPaymentsPaidToDate)
```

The first two functions (doPayment and doBalance)
  f.   take no parameters
  g.   are called from an onclick attribute
  h.   get input from the user
  i.   call the computePayment or the computeBalance function
  j.   display a result to the user

The computePayment function computes and returns the monthly payment for a loan with a fixed annual interest rate. The formula for computing a loan payment is

$$p = \frac{ar}{1 - (1+r)^{-n}}$$

Loan Calculator

Amount borrowed (principal)	80000
Annual interest rate (example: .065)	0.05
Number of years	30
Payments per year	12
Compute payment	$429.46
Number of payments paid to date	180
Compute payoff amount	$54306.40

Figure 9-7: The user interface for a loan calculator.

where p is the payment per period, a is the loan amount, r is the interest rate **per period**, and n is the total number of periods **throughout the life of the loan**.

The computeBalance function computes and returns the balance for a loan with a fixed annual interest rate. The formula for computing the balance of a loan after d payments have been made is

$$b = a(1+r)^d - \frac{p((1+r)^d - 1)}{r}$$

where b is the balance, a is the loan amount, r is the interest rate **per period**, p is the payment per period, and d is the number of payments **paid to date**.

Chapter 10. Arrays

An **array** is a collection of variables where each variable has the same data type, for example, an array of integers or an array of Student objects. Each variable in an array is called an **element** and has an **index**, also called the **subscript**, which denotes that element's location within the array. One advantage of using arrays is that all the elements within an array can be declared, created, or passed to a function as a whole. However, each element may still be accessed individually by using the element's index. Figure 10-1 shows a representation of an array with 10 elements.

Notice that each element has a unique index, and in JavaScript, indexes are always non-negative integers with 0 as the first index.

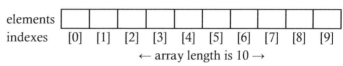

Figure 10-1: A representation of an array showing the elements and indexes.

Chapter Outcomes

By the end of this chapter, you will be able to:

- Declare, create, and populate an array.
- Write code to access a single value within an array.
- Write a loop to process every element in an array.
- Write code to sort and search an array.
- Use the methods in the Array object to process arrays.

Declaring an Array

Just like a variable must be declared before it can be used in a program, an array must also be declared. To declare an array in JavaScript, a programmer writes the keyword var followed by the array's name, exactly the same as declaring a variable.

Template

```
var arrayName;
```

Example 1

```
var data;
var scores;
```

Creating an Array

Declaring an array in JavaScript does not cause the computer to reserve space for the elements of the array. To do this, a programmer must also create the array. All objects, including arrays, are created in JavaScript using the keyword new.

Template

```
arrayName = new Array(size);
```

Example 2

```
data = new Array(6);
scores = new Array(25);
```

In the previous example, the first line causes the computer to reserve space for an array that holds six values with indexes numbered from 0 to 5 inclusive. The second line causes the computer to reserve space for an array named scores that holds 25 values numbered from 0 to 24 inclusive. It is possible to combine the array declaration and creation into a single statement.

Example 3

```
var data = new Array(6);
var scores = new Array(25);
```

Example 4

Declare and create an array named altitudes that has 50 elements in it.

var altitudes = new Array(50);

It is also possible to declare, create, and initialize the elements in an array in a single JavaScript statement.

Template

```
var arrayName = [ value0, value1, … valueN ];
```

Example 5

```
var measures = [ 4.7, -3, 2.1, 0, 7.2 ];
```

Example 6

Declare and create an array named degrees that has these numbers inside it: 25.2, 18.0, 31.6, 22.1

var degrees = [25.2, 18.0, 31.6, 22.1]

Array Length

All arrays in JavaScript automatically have an attribute named `length`, which is the number of elements contained in the array.

Template

```
arrayName.length
```

Example 7

```
var data = new Array(8);
var sizes = [ 4.7, 5.8, 2.1, 3.9, 7.2 ];
document.getElementById('div1').innerHTML = data.length;    // displays 8
document.getElementById('div2').innerHTML = sizes.length;   // displays 5
```

Accessing an Element

To access a single element within an array, either to read or to write the element's value, simply write the name of the array followed by the index of the element in brackets. In JavaScript, an index is always a non-negative integer, the first index is always 0, and the last index is always one less than the length of an array (*arrayName*. length − 1). An index is never a fractional number because it doesn't make sense to ask what is stored in an array at a fractional index, for example 3.8. There is a value stored at index 3 and a value stored at index 4 but nothing stored at index 3.8.

Template

```
arrayName[index]
```

Example 8

```
var data = new Array(6);
data[0] = -4.3;
data[1] = parseFloat(document.getElementById('input1').value);
⋮
document.getElementById('output').innerHTML = data[4];
⋮
if (data[5] > 6.3) {
    document.getElementById('error').innerHTML =
            'Data value is too high!';
}
```

Example 9

Write a statement to store the number 72.6 in an array named ranges at location 3.

Filling an Array

It is often desirable to have the computer initialize all the elements in an array to some value (usually zero). We do this by writing a statement that assigns a value to one element in the array, and then put that assignment statement inside a loop. If the array has *n* elements in it, then the loop causes the computer to repeat the assignment statement *n* times, once for each element in the array.

Example 10 contains a function that fills an array with some value x. Of course, in order for a computer to execute the code in the function, a programmer must write code to call the function, similar to this code:

```
var list = new Array(80);
fill(list, 7);
```

which creates an array with 80 elements and calls the `fill` function to store the number 7 in each element of the array.

Example 10

```
// Fills the specified array with the value x.
function fill(list, x) {
    // For each index in the array named list
    for (var i = 0; i < list.length; i++) {
        // store the value in x in the array
        list[i] = x;
    }
}
```

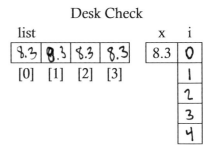

Filling an Array with a Ramp

Within programs that perform image processing, a computer uses an array as a **palette** or **look up table**. To get the color value of a pixel, the computer reads the value of the pixel stored in the image and then looks up that value in the palette. Then the computer displays the color from the palette at the corresponding pixel location on the monitor. Often the palette must be initialized to contain values that are constantly increasing, for example: 0, 1, 2, 3... This is known as a ramp because if you plotted the values in the array, you would see a sloping line or ramp, constantly increasing to the right as shown in Figure 10-2.

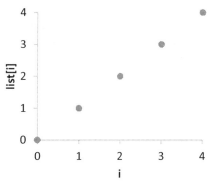

Figure 10-2: A plot of constantly increasing values forming a ramp.

Here is a code example showing how to initialize an array to an increasing ramp.

Example 11

```
// Fills the specified array with constantly increasing
// values from 0 to list.length - 1, inclusive.
function ramp(list) {
    for (var i = 0;  i < list.length;  i++) {
        list[i] = i;
    }
}
```

Desk Check

list

0	1	2	3	4
[0]	[1]	[2]	[3]	[4]

i

0
1
2
3
4
5

Occasionally we want to initialize an array to hold constantly decreasing values such as:
15, 14, 13 … 0. This is known as a reverse ramp because if you plotted the values in the array, you would see a sloping line or ramp, constantly decreasing to the right as shown in figure 15. Example code to initialize an array to a reverse ramp is shown below.

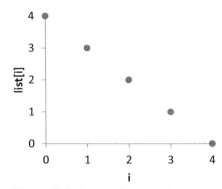

Figure 10-3: A plot of constantly decreasing values forming a reverse ramp.

Example 12

```
// Fills the specified array with constantly decreasing
// values from list.length - 1 to 0, inclusive.
function reverseRamp(list) {
    var high = list.length - 1;
    for (var i = 0;  i < list.length;  i++) {
        list[i] = high - i;
    }
}
```

Desk Check

list   high   i

| [0] | [1] | [2] | [3] | [4] |

Reversing an Array

Reversing the order of the elements in an array is not commonly used in computer programs. However, it is an interesting operation and understanding it helps students to understand more commonly used array operations. One way to reverse the elements in an array is to use two index variables, one index starts at the beginning of the array, and the other starts at the end of the array. Then write a loop that repeats $n / 2$ times where n is the number of elements in the array. Each time through the loop, the computer switches one element in the left half of the array with one element in the right half.

Example 13

```
// Reverses the contents of the specified array.
function reverse(list) {
    var left = 0;
    var right = list.length -1;

    while (left < right) {
        // Exchange two elements.
        var swap = list[left];
        list[left] = list[right];
        list[right] = swap;

        // Move the indexes toward the center.
        left++;
        right--;
    }
}
```

Desk Check

list

3.4	−2	5	7	12
[0]	[1]	[2]	[3]	[4]

left	right	swap

Summing the Values in an Array

Within a program, we often have a series of numbers stored in an array, and the program needs to calculate the sum of those numbers. This is easily done by writing a function with a variable to hold the sum and a loop that adds each value in an array to that variable.

Example 14

```
// Returns the sum of the values stored in an array.
function sum(list) {
    var s = 0;
    for (var i = 0; i < list.length; i++) {
        s += list[i];
    }
    return s;
}
```

Desk Check

list

3.4	-2	5	7	12
[0]	[1]	[2]	[3]	[4]

i	s

Finding a Value (Linear Search)

Very often a computer program must determine if a certain value is stored in an array or not and if stored in the array, then return the value's location. The value to be found is called the *key*. If the array is not too large (perhaps less than 100 elements), finding the key can be easily done using a linear search. A linear search is done by comparing each element in the array with the key until the key is found in the array or the end of the array is reached.

The advantage of a linear search is that it is simple and easy to code. The disadvantage is that it is too slow if the array has many elements in it. When the array has many elements in it, it is probably faster to sort the array and keep it sorted and to use a binary search to find the key within the array.

JavaScript code to perform a linear search is shown below. In the example, if the key is found in the array, the search function returns the index of the location within the array where the key was found. If the key is not found, the search function returns −1.

Example 15

```
// If key is in list, returns the first index where
// key is located within list; otherwise returns -1.
function linearSearch(list, key) {
    for (var i = 0;  i < list.length;  i++) {
        if (list[i] == key) {
            return i;
        }
    }
    return -1;
}
```

Desk Check

list						key	i	return
28.1	20	23.6	0	15		23.6		
[0]	[1]	[2]	[3]	[4]				

Parallel Arrays

Parallel arrays are two or more arrays that contain corresponding values. For example, an array of student IDs and an array of corresponding student names are parallel arrays. Consider this student data.

Student ID	Student Name
07-153-4276	Felix
34-513-3186	Jonathan
26-430-0198	Grace

We could store this data in a program in two parallel arrays like this.

```
var studentIDs = [ '07-153-4276', '34-513-3186', '26-430-0198' ];
var studentNames = [ 'Felix', 'Jonathan', 'Grace' ];
```

Programming Fundamentals in JavaScript

The arrays are parallel because the order for both arrays is the same. In other words, Felix's ID is stored at index 0 in the studentIDs array, and his name is stored also at index 0 in the studentNames array. Jonathan's ID is stored at index 1 and his name is stored at index 1, and so on. Here is a JavaScript program that reads a student ID from a text field and finds and outputs the corresponding student name. This program uses the two parallel arrays given above.

Example 16

```
<!DOCTYPE HTML>
<html lang="en-us">
<head>
<meta charset="utf-8">
<title>Student ID to Name</title>
<script>
// The values in these parallel arrays can be hard coded into a
// program, or even better, they can be read from a file or database.
var studentIDs = [ '07-153-4276', '26-430-0198', '34-513-3186' ];
var studentNames = [ 'Felix', 'Jonathan', 'Grace' ];

/* Input: a student's ID
 * Processing: find the student's name
 * Output: the student's name
 */
function findName() {
    // Get the student's ID.
    var studID = document.getElementById('studID').value;

    // Use linear search to find the student's ID.
    var index = linearSearch(studentIDs, studID);

    var name;
    if (index == -1) {
        // The student ID that the user entered
        // is not stored in the studentIDs array.
        name = 'No such student ID';
    }
    else {
        // Get the student's name.
        name = studentNames[index];
    }

    // Display the student's name for the user to see.
    document.getElementById('output').innerHTML = name;
}
```

Desk Check

studentIDs

"07-153-4276"	"34-513-3186"	"26-430-0198"
[0]	[1]	[2]

studentNames

"Felix"	"Jonathan"	"Grace"
[0]	[1]	[3]

```
// If key is in list, returns the first index where
// key is located within list; otherwise returns -1.
function linearSearch(list, key) {
    var index = -1;
    for (var i = 0;  i < list.length;  i++) {
        if (list[i] == key) {
            index = i;
            break;
        }
    }
    return index;
}
</script>
</head>

<body>
Student ID: <input type="text" id="studID">
<button type="button" onclick="findName()">Name</button>
<div id="output"></div>
</body>
</html>
```

key	i	index

Finding a Range

Sometimes a computer program has a list of numerical ranges and must find the range that contains some value. Examples of this type of computing problem include:

- determining a person's income tax rate from a list of income ranges and graduated tax rates
- determining a customer's discount rate from a list of purchase ranges and discount rates
- determining a salesperson's commission from a list of sales ranges and commission rates
- determining a student's letter grade from a list of score ranges and letter grades

For example, a company may offer discounts to its customers where the discount rate is based on the amount purchased according to this table.

If the purchase amount is greater than or equal to	And the purchase amount is less than	Then the discount rate is
0	$300	0%
$300	$600	2.0%
$600	$1000	2.5%
$1000	∞	3.0%

A beginning programmer will often code a JavaScript solution to this problem like this:

Example 17

```
// Computes and returns a discounted purchase amount.
function getDiscountedAmount(purchase) {
    var rate = 0;
    if (purchase >= 0 && purchase < 300) {
        rate = 0;
    }
    if (purchase >= 300 && purchase < 600) {
        rate = 0.02;
    }
    if (purchase >= 600 && purchase < 1000) {
        rate = 0.025;
    }
    if (purchase >= 1000) {
        rate = 0.03;
    }
    var discount = purchase * rate;
    return purchase - discount;
}
```

Desk Check

purchase	rate	discount	return
$708.00			

After a little practice, the beginning programmer realizes that the separate if statements can be connected with else and that the else part of each if statement will be executed only when the previous if part is false. This means the code can be written more succinctly and achieve exactly the same results by removing the left half of each if statement.

Example 18

```
// Computes and returns a discounted purchase amount.
function getDiscountedAmount(purchase) {
    var rate;
    if (purchase < 300) {
        rate = 0;
    }
    else if (purchase < 600) {
        rate = 0.02;
    }
    else if (purchase < 1000) {
        rate = 0.025;
    }
    else {
        rate = 0.03;
    }
    var discount = purchase * rate;
    return purchase - discount;
}
```

Desk Check

purchase	rate	discount	return
$708.00			

The problem with both these solutions is that if the company changes the purchase amount ranges or the discount rates, then a programmer must change the corresponding code. An improved solution is to remove the ranges and rates from the code and place them in a file or database so that the computer can read them into an array when it runs the program. Then the programmer must write a simple linear search method to find the correct range and the corresponding discount rate as shown in the next example.

Example 19

```
// The values in these arrays can be hard coded
// into your program, or even better, they can
// be read from a file or a database.
var limits = [ 300, 600, 1000 ];
var rates = [ 0, 0.02, 0.025, 0.03 ];

// Computes and returns a discounted purchase amount.
function getDiscountedAmount(purchase) {

    // Find the purchase range.
    for (var i = 0;  i < limits.length;  i++) {
        if (purchase < limits[i]) {
            break;
        }
    }

    // Get the discount rate that
    // corresponds to the purchase range.
    var rate = rates[i];

    //
    var discount = purchase * rate;
    return purchase - discount;
}
```

Desk Check

limits

300	600	1000
[0]	[1]	[2]

rates

0	0.02	0.025	0.03
[0]	[1]	[2]	[3]

purchase	i	rate	discount	return
$708.00				

The next code example is a complete program that includes the getDiscountedAmount function from the previous example.

Example 20

```
<!DOCTYPE HTML>
<html lang="en-us">
<head>
<meta charset="utf-8">
<title>Compute Total</title>
<script>
/* Input: The subtotal for a customer's purchases
 * Processing: Compute a discounted amount and sales tax and add
 *      them together to get the total amount that the customer owes.
 * Output: The total that the customer owes.
 */
function computeTotal() {
    // Get the subtotal from the user.
    var subtotal = parseFloat(document.getElementById('subtotal').value);

    // Compute the customer's total.
    var discounted = getDiscountedAmount(subtotal);
    var tax = getSalesTax(discounted);
    var total = discounted + tax;

    // Display the total for the customer to see.
    document.getElementById('total').innerHTML = total;
}


// The values in these parallel arrays can be
// hard coded into your program, or even better,
// they can be read from a file or database.
var limits = [ 300, 600, 1000 ];
var rates = [ 0, 0.02, 0.025, 0.03 ];

// Computes and returns a discounted purchase amount.
function getDiscountedAmount(purchase) {
    // Find the purchase range.
    for (var i = 0;  i < limits.length;  i++) {
        if (purchase < limits[i]) {
            break;
        }
    }

    // Get the discount rate that
    // corresponds to the purchase range.
    var rate = rates[i];

    // Compute the discount amount and round it to pennies.
    var discount = purchase * rate;
    discount = roundToPlaces(discount, 2);

    // Compute and return the discounted price.
    return purchase - discount;
}
```

```
// Computes and returns the sales tax for a purchase amount.
function getSalesTax(purchase) {
    var taxRate = 0.06;
    var tax = purchase * taxRate;
    tax = roundToPlaces(tax, 2);
    return tax;
}


// Rounds x to digits places after the decimal.
function roundToPlaces(x, digits) {
    var multiplier = Math.pow(10, digits);
    var rounded = Math.round(x * multiplier) / multiplier;
    return rounded;
}
</script>
</head>

<body>
<h2>Compute Total</h2>
Subtotal <input type="text" id="subtotal" size="5"><br>
<button type="button" onclick="computeTotal()">Total</button>
<div id="total"></div>
</body>
</html>
```

Finding a Value (Binary Search)

If the elements in an array are sorted, then the computer can use a faster algorithm called **binary search** to find an element within that array. The binary search algorithm works by comparing the key to the middle most element in the array. If the key is greater than the middle most element, then the search is repeated in the last half of the array. If the key is less than the middle most element, then the search is repeated in the first half of the array. Of course, if the key is equal to the middle most element, then the key has been found and the search is done. This process of comparing the key to the middle most element of the current interval is repeated until the key is found or the interval has shrunk to only one element. If that one element is not the same as the key, then the key is not present in the array, and the function below returns a negative value.

Example 21

```
// If key is in list, returns any index where key is
// located within list; otherwise returns -insertPoint - 1.
// Assumes list is already sorted.
function binarySearch(list, key) {
    var left = 0;
    var right = list.length - 1;
    while (left <= right) {
        // Compute the index of the middle of the current interval.
        var mid = left + ((right - left) >>> 1);

        // Compare the value in the middle of the interval to the key.
        var cmp = key - list[mid];
        if (cmp > 0) {
            left = mid + 1;
        }
        else if (cmp < 0) {
            right = mid - 1;
        }
        else {
            return mid;
        }
    }

    // key is not present in list, but if it
    // were, it would be stored at location left.
    return -(left + 1);
}
```

Desk Check

list

−2.1	−1	3.9	6.2	7.1	9.7	10	12	13.1	15.6	18	19	20.1	24.5
[0]	[1]	[2]	[3]	[4]	[5]	[6]	[7]	[8]	[9]	[10]	[11]	[12]	[13]

key	left	right	mid	cmp	return
15.6					

If the key is not present in the array, the return value of the binary search function above is -insertPoint - 1. In other words, if the key is not present in the array, the index where key should be inserted can be found using this code:

```
var index = binarySearch(list, key);
if (index < 0) {
    var insertPoint = -index - 1;
}
```

In the `binarySearch` code above, the statement that computes *mid* needs some explanation. Here is the statement:

```
mid = left + ((right - left) >>> 1);
```

The right shift operator (>>>) shifts all the bits in an integer to the right which is the same as using integer division to divide a *non-negative* integer by a power of two. However, the right shift operator executes faster than division. To help us understand the statement, we can rewrite it by replacing >>> 1 with / 2.

```
mid = left + Math.floor((right - left) / 2);
```

Notice that this statement uses the `Math.floor` function to truncate (not round) the result of the division. Also, notice that if this were an algebraic expression, it could be simplified to

```
mid = Math.floor((left + right) / 2);
```

which is easier to understand. From this simplified formula, we see that the midpoint is simply the left index plus the right index divided in half. However, because of number overflow, if we use the simplified formula in the code, it may not work for very large arrays, and so we must use the more complex formula.

Array Methods

JavaScript includes several useful methods that you can use to manipulate the contents of arrays. Many of these methods are listed in the next table. When calling these methods, a programmer must write the name of the array in front of the method name as shown in this template.

Template

```
arrayName.methodName(arg1, arg2, … argN);
```

Array Methods

Method	Description
`a.concat(item1, item2, …)`	Returns a new array composed of the original array and the argument arrays or values.
`a.every(func, thisArg)`	Returns true if a test function returns true for every element in an array.
`a.filter(func, thisArg)`	Returns a new array that contains all elements that passed a test function.
`a.forEach(func, thisArg)`	Calls a function once for each element in an array.
`a.indexOf(toFind, start)`	Returns the index within the array *a* of the first occurrence of the element *toFind*, or -1 if not found.
`a.join(separator)`	Joins all elements of an array into a string.
`a.lastIndexOf(toFind, start)`	Returns the index within the array *a* of the last occurrence of the element *toFind*, or -1 if not found.

Programming Fundamentals in JavaScript

Array Methods

Method	Description
`a.map(func, thisArg)`	Returns a new array that contains the results of calling a function on every element in an array.
`a.pop()`	Removes and returns the last element from an array.
`a.push(item1, item2, …)`	Adds one or more elements to the end of an array.
`a.reduce(func, thisArg)`	Returns an accumulated value produced by calling a function on every element in an array.
`a.reverse()`	Reverses the elements in an array.
`a.shift()`	Removes and returns the first element from an array.
`a.slice(start, end)`	Returns a new array that is a copy of elements between [*start*, *end*).
`a.some(func, thisArg)`	Returns true if a test function returns true for at least one element in an array.
`a.sort(compareFunc)`	Sorts the elements of an array in place.
`a.toString()`	Returns a string representing an array.
`a.splice(start, count, item1, item2, …)`	Removes and adds elements to an array. ☆
`a.unshift(item1, item2, …)`	Adds one or more elements to the beginning of an array.

Sorting an Array

The best way to sort an array is to use the sort functionality provided by the programming language you are using because this built in sorting functionality has been optimized and tested. JavaScript includes built in sort functionality, which is in the Array object. Shown below is JavaScript code to sort an array using the built in functionality.

```
var vegetables = [ "Radish", "Carrot", "Tomato", "Pea" ];
vegetables.sort();
```

If you wish to sort elements in a different order than the one provided by the JavaScript language, then you must write a comparison function and pass that function as a parameter to the sort function. This next JavaScript example shows how to sort text strings in descending order.

Example 22

```
/* Compares two values, s1 and s2 and returns -1
 * if s1 should come before s2, 1 if s1 should come
 * after s2, and 0 if the two values are equal. */
function descend(s1, s2) {
    if (s1 > s2)
        return -1;
    if (s1 < s2)
        return 1;
    return 0;
}

var vegetables = [ "Radish", "Carrot", "Tomato", "Pea" ];
vegetables.sort(descend);
```

The next example is a complete program that gets a list of text items from a user, sorts the list, and outputs the sorted list. This program allows a user to enter a list in a text area instead of a text field. A text area is essentially a text field with multiple rows. This program uses the built-in split function to split the string that the user enters into an array. This program also uses the built-in sort function to sort the array of text items and the built-in join function to join the sorted array into a string. The running program is shown in Figure 10-4.

Figure 10-4: A JavaScript program that reads a list of text items, sorts the list, and outputs the sorted list.

Example 23

```
<!DOCTYPE HTML>
<html lang="en-us">
<head>
<meta charset="utf-8">
<meta name="author" content="Rex Barzee">
<title>Sort Text</title>

<script>
/* Input: A list of text items, each item on a separate line.
 * Processing:
 *      Split the text items into an array.
 *      Sort the array.
 *      Join the array into a string.
 * Output: The sorted list of text items
 */
function process() {
    // Get the text entered by the user.
    var text = document.getElementById('input').value;

    // Split the text at each new
    // line into an array of strings.
    var list = text.split('\n');

    // Sort the array of strings.
    list.sort();

    // Join the sorted array into a string
    // of text separated by newline characters.
    var output = list.join('\n');

    // Display the string for the user to see.
    document.getElementById('output').value = output;
}
</script>
</head>

<body>
<textarea id="input" rows="16" cols="20"></textarea>
<button type="button" onclick="process()">Sort</button>
<textarea id="output" rows="16" cols="20"></textarea>
</body>
</html>
```

Sorting Numbers

By default the built in sort function in JavaScript sorts arrays lexicographically which essentially means alphabetically. This causes problems if you wish to sort an array of numbers. For example, this code will sort the *numbers* array in a surprising way.

```
var numbers = [ 7, 10, 8, 16, 3, 35 ];

// WARNING: this will sort the numbers array
// alphabetically and not numerically.
numbers.sort();
```

In the previous code, after the computer calls the sort function, the values in the *numbers* array will be [10, 16, 3, 35, 7, 8]. By default, the built in JavaScript sort function places 10 and 16 before 3, 7, and 8 because 10 and 16 begin with 1 and lexicographically 1 comes before 3, 7, and 8. To force JavaScript to sort an array according to its numeric values, we have to pass a comparison function into the sort function.

Example 24

```
<!DOCTYPE HTML>
<html lang="en-us">
<head>
<meta charset="utf-8">
<title>Compound Interest</title>

<script>
/* Input: No user input
 * Processing: Test the built-in JavaScript sort function
 * Output: The contents of an array before it is
 *      sorted, and the contents after it is sorted.
 */
function testSort() {
    var numbers = [ 7, 10, 8, 16, 3, 35 ];
    document.getElementById('output').innerHTML = numbers + '<br>';
    numbers.sort(compareNumbers);
    document.getElementById('output').innerHTML += numbers;
}

/* Compares two numbers by subtracting the second from the
 * first which will return a negative number if the first
 * number should be placed before the second, a zero if the
 * two numbers are equal, and a positive number if the first
 * number should be placed after the second. */
function compareNumbers(x, y) {
    return x - y;
}
</script>
</head>

<body>
```

Programming Fundamentals in JavaScript

```
<button type="button" onclick="testSort()">Sort an Array</button>
<div id="output"></div>
</body>
</html>
```

You might be wondering how a sort function works. There are many different, well known sort algorithms (selection, exchange, insertion, heap, quick, etc.). They all work by repeatedly comparing elements in an array to other elements in the array and simply moving the elements around within the array. Shown below is JavaScript code to sort an array using the insertion sort algorithm. Insertion sort is a simple and reasonably fast algorithm, although it is usually not as fast as the quick sort algorithm.

Example 25

```
// Sorts the contents of the specified array in
// ascending order using the insertion sort algorithm.
function sort(list) {
    var first = 0;
    var last = list.length - 1;
    for (var i = last - 1;  i >= first;  i--) {
        var swap = list[i];
        for (var j = i + 1;  j <= last;  j++) {
            if (swap <= list[j]) {
                break;
            }
            list[j - 1] = list[j];
        }
        list[j - 1] = swap;
    }
}
```

Desk Check

list

6	−8	9	7	0
6	−8	9		

6	−8			

6		0	7	9

			7	9
[0]	[1]	[2]	[3]	[4]

first last i swap j

Common Mistakes

Forgetting that the first index in a JavaScript array is always 0

Incorrect

```
for (var i = 1;  i < a.length;  i++) {
    a[i] = 0;
}
```

Correct

```
for (var i = 0;  i < a.length;  i++) {
    a[i] = 0;
}
```

Going beyond the end of an array

Incorrect

```
for (var i = 0;  i <= a.length;  i++) {
    a[i] = 0;
}
```

Correct

```
for (var i = 0;  i < a.length;  i++) {
    a[i] = 0;
}
```

Confusing an index with the value stored at an index

Incorrect
```
var sum = 0;
for (var i = 0; i < a.length; i++) {
    // Wrong! i is the index. This code ignores the
    // values that are stored in the array and simply
    // adds the indexes of the array which are the
    // integers 0, 1, 2, … (a.length - 1)
    sum += i;
}
```

Correct
```
var sum = 0;
for (var i = 0; i < a.length; i++) {
    // Right. a[i] is the value stored at index i.
    // This code adds the values that are stored
    // in the array.
    sum += a[i];
}
```

Chapter Summary

- An array is a collection of variables. Each variable in an array is called an element and has a unique index which denotes that element's location within the array

- To declare an array, use the keyword var.

- To create an array which will reserve space in main memory for the elements of the array, write code that uses the keywords new and Array, like this template:

  arrayName = new Array(*size*);

- To create and populate an array with known values write code that uses square brackets ([and]) like this template:

  arrayName = [*value0, value1, ... valueN*];

- All arrays in JavaScript automatically have an attribute named length, which is the number of elements contained in the array.

- To access a single element within an array either to read or write the element's value, use bracket notation:

  arrayName[*index*]

- The first index in a JavaScript array is always 0.

- The last index in a JavaScript array is always the length of the array minus 1 or in other words:

  var lastIndex = arrayName.length - 1;

- To process all the elements in an array, a programmer will usually write a loop that counts from zero to the length of the array similar to this:

  ```
  for (var i = 0;  i < arrayName.length;  i++) {
      // Process each element of array using i as the index.
  }
  ```

- JavaScript includes many built-in methods that process arrays, including concat, indexOf, join, lastIndexOf, pop, push, reverse, shift, and sort.

Review Questions

1. Given the following JavaScript statement, what is the index of the last element in the array named `stuff`?
    ```
    var stuff = [ 13, -1.8, 20, 6.3 ];
    ```

2. Given the following JavaScript statement what is the value of the last element in the array named `things`?
    ```
    var things = [ 13, -8, 12.1, 3.7 ];
    ```

3. Given the following array what is the value of s[3] - s[1]?
    ```
    var s = [ 4, -1, 0, 5, 9, 1, 2, 4 ];
    ```

4. Write JavaScript code to declare and create an array named `data` that has 75 elements.

5. Write JavaScript code to call the `fill` function as given in example 10 of this chapter and pass the array that you created in the previous review question to the `fill` function.

6. Write JavaScript code to declare and create an array named `samples` that holds these values 72, -3, 59, 0, 16.

7. Write code to output (display to the user) the value stored at index 1 in the `samples` array.

Programming Assignments

1. Write a function that creates and returns an array that contains the values: 1908, 5, 10. The function must have this header:

    ```
    function mothersDay()
    ```

2. Write a function that returns the sum of the first and last values in an array. The function must have this header:

    ```
    function addEnds(list)
    ```

    For example, if the `addEnds` function were called like this:

    ```
    var list = [ 17, 8, 9, 5, 20 ];
    var value = addEnds(list);
    ```

    the `addEnds` function would return 37 because 17 and 20 are the first and last values stored in the array, and the sum of 17 and 20 is 37.

3. Write a function named getMiddle that returns the value of the middle element in an array. If the array has an even number of elements, then this function must return the average of the two middle elements. The function must have this header:
    function getMiddle(list)

    For example, if the getMiddle function were called like this:
    var list = [17, 8, 9, 5, 20];
    var value = getMiddle(list);

    the getMiddle function would return 9 because 9 is stored in the middle of the array. If the getMiddle function were called like this:
    var list = [12, 4, 8, 15, 17, 5, 20, 11];
    var value = getMiddle(list);

    the getMiddle function would return 16 because 15 and 17 are stored in the middle of the array, and the average of 15 and 17 is 16.

4. Write a function named countEvens that counts and returns the number of even integers in an array. The function must have this header:
    function countEvens(list)

    For example, if the countEvens function were called like this:
    var list = [17, 8, 9, 5, 20];
    var count = countEvens(list);

    the countEvens function would return 2 because 8 and 20 are even integers.

5. Write a function to multiply each element in an array by some value. The function must have this header:
    function multiply(list, multiplier)

    For example, if the multiply function were called like this:
    var list = [17, 8, 9, 5, 20];
    var products = multiply(list, 3);

    the multiply function would return an array with these values: [51, 24, 27, 15, 60]

6. Write a function to rotate the elements in an array to the left. In other words, the function must move each element from its location to the location immediately to the left, and then move the first value from its location to the last location (not necessarily in that order). The function must have this header:
`function rotateLeft(list)`

For example, if the `rotateLeft` function were called like this:
```
var list = [ 17, 8, 9, 5, 20 ];
rotateLeft(list);
```

The `rotateLeft` function would change the `list` array to be `[ 8, 9, 5, 20, 17 ]`.

7. Write a function to rotate the elements in an array to the right. In other words, the function must move each element from its location to the location immediately to the right, and then move the last value from its location to the first location (not necessarily in that order). The function must have this header:
`function rotateRight(list)`

For example, if the `rotateRight` function were called like this:
```
var list = [ 17, 8, 9, 5, 20 ];
rotateRight(list);
```

The `rotateRight` function would change the list array to be `[ 20, 17, 8, 9, 5 ]`.

8. In the card game named **golf**, each player tries to collect cards with the lowest value. The game is usually played with a deck of cards that has four suits: spades, hearts, diamonds, and clubs. Each suit has 13 cards: 1, 2, 3, 4, 5, 6, 7, 8, 9, 10, Jack, Queen, and King. At the end of the game, each player calculates his score by adding the value of the cards that he holds in his hand. The value of the numbered cards is the same as their number. However, the value of a Jack, Queen, or King is 10. In some versions of the game, each player has four cards in his hand. In other versions, each player has six or eight cards in his hand.

Write a function named `golfScore` that takes onc parameter: an array named hand. This function must compute and return the score for the cards by adding the values of all the cards in hand. For example, if hand were this array: `[5, 2, "King", 3, 1, "Queen"]`, the `golfScore` function would return 31.

9. Write an HTML document with a button and a div. The onclick attribute of the button must call a function named crazyStory() with no arguments. The div must have an id of 'output'. Write these five functions in the head of the document, all in the same script tag:

```
function chooseNoun()
function chooseVerb()
function chooseAdjective()
function chooseAdverb()
function chooseInteger()
```

The first four functions must each contain an array with at least ten words. The chooseNoun function must contain an array with at least ten nouns. The chooseVerb function must contain an array with at least ten verbs, and so on. When one of these four functions is called, the function must randomly choose one of the words in its array and return that word. Hint: write code similar to example 10 of Chapter 9 to get a pseudo random index between 0 and the length of the array of words, in other words in this range [0, *length*). Then write code to return the word that is stored in the array at that index.

The last function, chooseInteger must return a pseudo random integer between 1 and 99, inclusive. Finally, add this function to the same script tag as the other five functions.

```
function crazyStory() {
    var story = "The man comes "
        + chooseVerb() + "ing a horse. The horse is "
        + chooseAdverb() + " " + chooseAdjective()
        + " and has no " + chooseNoun()
        + ". The saddle is " + chooseAdjective()
        + ", and the stirrups don't match. His clothing"
        + " is strange. He wears " + chooseInteger()
        + " hats and a " + chooseAdjective()
        + " shirt. One " + chooseNoun()
        + " of his pants is torn off to the knee. His sword is "
        + chooseAdjective() + " and has a broken hilt and "
        + chooseVerb() + "s from the bottom of the "
        + chooseNoun() + ".";
    document.getElementById('output').innerHTML = story;
}
```

10. *The Twelve Days of Christmas* is an English Christmas carol that lists a series of gifts given on each of the twelve days of Christmas. In the song, the gifts are listed cumulatively. This means on day one, the song lists the gift for day one. On day two, the song lists the gifts for day two and day one. On day three, the song lists the gifts for days three, two, and one and so on. These are the gifts for each of the twelve days:

Day	Gift
1	a partridge in a pear tree
2	two turtle doves
3	three French hens
4	four calling birds
5	five golden rings
6	six geese a laying
7	seven swans a swimming
8	eight maids a milking
9	nine ladies dancing
10	ten lords a leaping
11	eleven pipers piping
12	twelve drummers drumming

Write a program that allows a user to enter an integer between 1 and 12, inclusive and that displays the corresponding lyrics from *The Twelve Days of Christmas*. For example, if a user entered 1, your program should output:
"On the first day of Christmas, my true love gave to me: a partridge in a pear tree."

If the user entered 4, your program should output:
"On the fourth day of Christmas, my true love gave to me: four calling birds, three French hens, two turtle doves, and a partridge in a pear tree."

Hint: create an array that contains the ordinal numbers: first, second, third... and another array that contains the gifts. Use those arrays, a loop, and string concatenation to build a string that contains the lyrics.

11. Write an HTML document with two text areas and a button. Write a JavaScript program that will
    a. read all the text from the first text area,
    b. split the text into numbers in an array,
    c. sort the array, and
    d. display the sorted numbers in the second text area.

12. Write a JavaScript program that allows a user to enter a list of names in a text area. When the user clicks a button, the program should output the list of names without any duplicated names. In other words, the program should output each name once only. Hint: The program should read the names from the left text area and store them in an array. Then it should sort the array, remove the duplicate names from the array, and display the names in the right text area.

13. Here is an array that holds a representation of all the cards in a deck Rook cards.

```
var cards = [
    "Green 1", "Green 2", "Green 3", "Green 4", "Green 5",
    "Green 6", "Green 7", "Green 8", "Green 9", "Green 10",
    "Green 11", "Green 12", "Green 13", "Green 14",
    "Yellow 1", "Yellow 2", "Yellow 3", "Yellow 4", "Yellow 5",
    "Yellow 6", "Yellow 7", "Yellow 8", "Yellow 9", "Yellow 10",
    "Yellow 11", "Yellow 12", "Yellow 13", "Yellow 14",
    "Black 1", "Black 2", "Black 3", "Black 4", "Black 5",
    "Black 6", "Black 7", "Black 8", "Black 9", "Black 10",
    "Black 11", "Black 12", "Black 13", "Black 14",
    "Red 1", "Red 2", "Red 3", "Red 4", "Red 5",
    "Red 6", "Red 7", "Red 8", "Red 9", "Red 10",
    "Red 11", "Red 12", "Red 13", "Red 14", "Rook Bird"
];
```

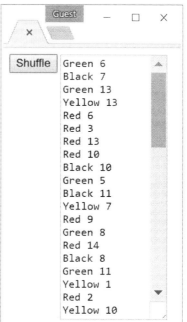

Read about the Fisher-Yates shuffle algorithm at wikipedia.org. Then write a JavaScript program that will shuffle the strings in the cards array and display the shuffled cards in a text area. Hint: find the "modern algorithm" that is shown about one fourth of the way down in the Wikipedia article. Translate this "modern algorithm" into JavaScript code.

14. Write a function that uses an array and no if statements to solve the Arabic number to Roman numerals programming assignment as given in chapter 6.

Chapter 11. Objects

When a programmer writes a large program, it is difficult for the programmer to keep all the code organized. One way to keep the code in a large program organized is to use object-oriented programming. **Object-oriented programming** is a way of viewing the world and designing and implementing software that matches the world.

Chapter Outcomes

By the end of this chapter, you will:

- Understand the terms object and class
- Understand object-oriented relationships aggregation, composition, inheritance, dependency, and association
- Understand multiplicities applied to aggregation, composition, and association
- Read a UML class diagram
- Create a JavaScript object from a built-in prototype object
- Add an attribute to a JavaScript object
- Read the value of an attribute from a JavaScript object
- Call a function from a JavaScript object
- Use a JavaScript object as a dictionary
- Store and retrieve data from the built-in localStorage object
- Understand how to change HTML elements in the document object model (DOM)

Objects and Classes

An **object** is anything in the world that has these four things:

Identity	A unique name or identification number
Data	These are characteristics of an object and are usually adjectives. These are also called attributes, properties, characteristics, fields, instance variables, or structure.
Behavior	These are the things that an object does and are usually verbs. These are also called methods, operations, functions, or procedures.
Relationships	links or connections between objects

A **class** is both a group of similar objects and a pattern for creating objects. Since an object has identity, data, behavior, and relationships and since a class is a pattern for creating objects, then a class must have those four things as well.

Unified Modeling Language

Many programmers use diagrams to design and document the classes and objects in their programs. The most common language used for these diagrams is the **Unified Modeling Language** (UML). One type of diagram in the UML is the **class diagram**. Figure 11-1 shows a UML class diagram with two classes. Within a class diagram, each class is shown as a rectangle usually with three sections. The first section contains the name of the class. The second section contains a list of the data that all objects created from the class will have. The third section contains a list of the behaviors that all objects created from the class will have.

Student
-firstName
-lastName
-address
-phone
+changeName()
+register()
+attendClass()
+withdraw()

Course
-number
-title
-description
-location
+open()
+allowStudent()
+close()

Figure 11-1: A UML class diagram showing two classes.

Relationships

There are several different relationships that can exist between objects or classes. Relationships between classes are shown as different types of lines connected to the classes.

Aggregation   A relationship between two objects such that one object contains the other object. This is sometimes called a whole-part relationship. In order to use aggregation between two objects *whole* and *part*, one of these English phrases must make sense: *whole* contains *part* or *whole* has a *part*. The UML symbol for aggregation is a solid line with an unfilled diamond connected to the containing class:

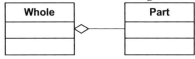

Composition   A relationship between two objects such that one object contains the other object and the contained object may not be shared. This is also a whole-part relationship and is a strong form of aggregation. In order to use composition between two objects *whole* and *part*, one of these English phrases must make sense: *whole* contains *part* or *whole* has a *part*. The UML symbol for aggregation is a solid line with a filled diamond connected to the containing class:

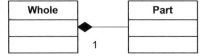

Inheritance   A relationship between two classes that causes the child class to automatically have everything (data, behavior, and relationships) that the parent class has. In order to use inheritance between two objects *parent* and *child*, one of these English phrases must make sense: *child* is a kind of *parent* or *child* is a *parent*. The UML symbol for inheritance is a solid line with an unfilled triangle connected to the parent class.

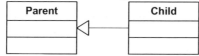

Dependency   A relationship between two objects such that one object requires or uses the other object to accomplish a task. In order to use dependency between two objects *x* and *y*, one of these English phrases must make sense: *x* uses *y*, *x* requires *y*, or *x* needs *y*. The UML symbol for dependency is a dashed line with an open arrow head connected to the required or needed class.

Association   A general relationship between objects. When two objects are related but the relationship is not aggregation, composition, inheritance, or dependency, then use association. The UML symbol for association is a solid line.

Multiplicities

Multiplicities are small numbers and punctuation at one or both ends of a relationship that constrain the relationship. A single number multiplicity constrains a relationship to exactly that number of objects. Two or more numbers separated by commas constrain a relationship to exactly one of those numbers of objects. Two numbers separated by two periods (..) constrain a relationship to a range of objects. For example, multiplicities may be used to show that one egg carton has either 12 or 18 eggs inside it as shown in Figure 11-2.

Figure 11-2: A UML class diagram showing two classes with multiplicities.

Multiplicity Examples

Multiplicity	Meaning
1	Exactly one
4,8	Exactly four or exactly eight
0,1	Zero or one, also known as optional
0..1	Zero or one, also known as optional
12..18	Between 12 and 18 inclusive
0..*	Zero or more
*	Zero or more
1..*	One or more, also known as at least one
3..*	Three or more, also known as at least three

Example 1

Label the parts of this UML class diagram, including class, attributes, operations, aggregation, composition, inheritance, association, and multiplicities.

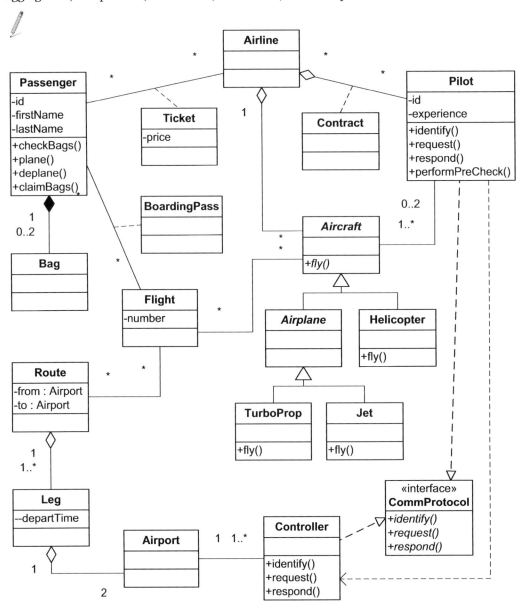

Figure 11-3: A UML class diagram for an airline.

Example 2

The following diagram shows many of the elements of the JavaScript programming language and the relationships among those elements. The relationships are shown using UML symbols.

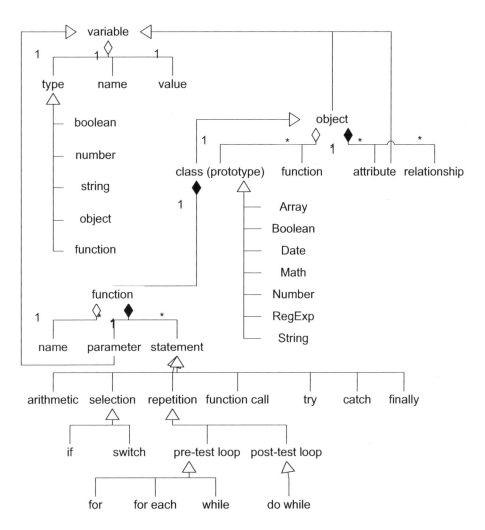

Figure 11-4: Elements of the JavaScript language and the relationships among those elements.

JavaScript Built-in Objects

Following is a list of the JavaScript prototype objects that a programmer can use to create new objects and a list of other JavaScript objects that a programmer can use in a program.

JavaScript Prototype Objects

Object Name	Purpose
Array	Stores multiple values as a single variable
Boolean	Stores either true or false
Date	Stores a date and time
Number	Stores a numeric value
String	Stores text
RegExp	Used to match patterns in text

Other JavaScript Objects

Object Name	Purpose
Math	Contains constants and functions used in calculations
window	An open window in a browser where an HTML document is displayed to the user
document	The HTML document that is open in a window

Declaring an Object

Just like a variable must be declared before it can be used in a program, an object must also be declared. To declare an object in JavaScript, a programmer writes the keyword var followed by the object's name, exactly the same as declaring a variable.

Template

```
var objName, objName2, … objNameN;
```

Example 3

```
var now;
var s;
```

Creating an Object

Declaring an object in JavaScript does not cause the computer to reserve space in memory for the attributes of the object. To do this, a programmer must also create the object. All objects are created in JavaScript using the keyword new. In many programming languages, a programmer must write the name of a class after the new keyword. However, JavaScript doesn't have classes, but instead has prototype objects. So, after writing the new keyword, a JavaScript programmer must write a prototype object's name.

Template

```
objectName = new PrototypeName(arg1, arg2, … argN);
```

Example 4

```
now = new Date();
s = new String();
```

In the previous example, the first line of code causes the computer to create a `Date` object that will hold the date and time of the moment that it is created in the computer's memory. The second line causes the computer to create an empty `String` object. It is possible to combine an object declaration and creation into a single statement.

Example 5

```
var now = new Date();
var date = new Date('2015/04/25');
var s = new String();
var n = new Number(103.7);
```

It is also possible to declare, create, and initialize an object in a single JavaScript statement.

Template

```
var objectName = { attrib1Name : value1, attrib2Name : value2 … };
```

Example 6

```
var student = {firstName:'Samuel', address:'125 W Main', height:1.78};
```

student : Object
firstName = 'Samuel'
address = '125 W Main'
height = 1.78

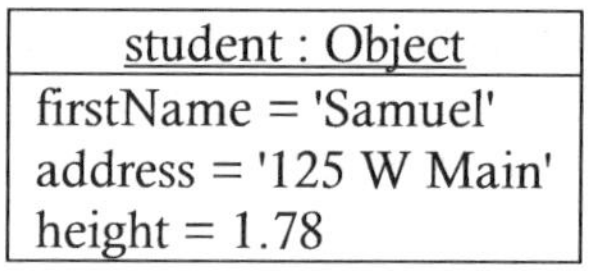

Figure 11-5: A UML object diagram showing one object.

Accessing an Attribute

To access an attribute of an object, either to write or to read the attribute's value, simply write the name of the object followed by a period (.) followed by the name of the attribute.

Template

```
objectName.attributeName
```

Example 7

```
// Store 'Jill' in a student object's firstName attribute.
student.firstName = 'Jill';

// Read the firstName attribute from a student object.
var f = student.firstName;
```

Calling a Method

A **method** is a function that is part of an object. To call a method, simply write the name of the object, a period (.), the name of the function, and an argument list.

Template

```
objectName.funcName(arg1, arg2, … argN);
```

Example 8

```
var date = new Date();
date.setFullYear(2025);
var s = date.toDateString();
```

Dictionaries

Because JavaScript stores attributes in objects as name value pairs, a programmer can use a JavaScript object as a dictionary. A **dictionary** is a collection of key value pairs where each key appears only once. A computer can insert and remove key value pairs from a dictionary and can search a dictionary very quickly. A dictionary is sometimes called an associative array or a map. One example of a program that could use a dictionary is a program that finds a student's name by using her student ID. Example 16 in chapter 10 solves this problem using parallel arrays. The following example solves the same problem using an object as a dictionary.

Example 9

```
<!DOCTYPE HTML>
<html lang="en-us">
<head>
<meta charset="utf-8">
<title>Student ID to Name</title>
<script>
// The values in this dictionary can be hard coded into a program
// or even better, they can be read from a file or database.
var students = {
    '07-153-4276' : 'Felix',
    '34-513-3186' : 'Jonathan',
    '26-430-0198' : 'Grace'
};
```

```
/* Input: a student's ID
 * Processing: find the student's name
 * Output: the student's name
 */
function findName() {
    // Get the student's ID.
    var studID = document.getElementById('studID').value;

    // Find the student's name in the dictionary of students.
    var name = students[studID];
    if (!name) {
        // The student ID that the user entered
        // is not stored in the students array.
        name = 'No such student ID';
    }

    // Display the student's name for the user to see.
    document.getElementById('output').innerHTML = name;
}
</script>
</head>

<body>
Student ID: <input type="text" id="studID">
<button type="button" onclick="findName()">Name</button>
<div id="output"></div>
</body>
</html>
```

Local Storage

Sometimes a programmer needs to store data that persists after a program finishes. One way to do this in JavaScript is to use local storage. **localStorage** is a built-in JavaScript object that holds data after a program finishes and even after a user closes the browser. To store a value in local storage, a programmer simply adds an attribute to the localStorage object.

Template

```
localStorage.attributeName = value;
```

To retrieve a value from local storage, a programmer uses the same attribute that he used to store the data.

Template

```
var varName = localStorage.attributeName;
```

Example 10

This small example program stores a user's name to local storage in the `saveName` function and reads a user's a name from local storage using the `loadName` function.

```
<!DOCTYPE HTML>
<html lang="en-us">
<head>
<meta charset="utf-8">
<title>Local Storage Demo</title>
<script>
/* Saves the user's name to local storage. */
function saveName() {
    var name = document.getElementById('name').value;
    localStorage.name = name;
}


/* Loads the user's name from local storage. */
function loadName() {
    var name = localStorage.name;
    document.getElementById('name').value = name;
}


/* Builds and shows a message to a user. */
function showMessage() {
    // Get the user's name from the text field.
    var name = document.getElementById('name').value;

    // Build a message for the user.
    var message;
    if (name == "") {
        message = 'Please enter your name.';
    }
    else {
        message = 'Hello ' + name + '. I hope you have nice day.';
    }

    // Display the message for the user to see.
    document.getElementById('output').innerHTML = message;
}
</script>
</head>

<body>
Name: <input type="text" id="name">
<button type="button" onclick="loadName()">Load</button>
<button type="button" onclick="saveName()">Save</button><br>
<button type="button" onclick="showMessage()">Message</button>
<div id="output"></div>
</body>
</html>
```

Document Object Model

JavaScript was developed so that HTML pages could be interactive, meaning that they could change as a user moved her mouse pointer and clicked the mouse buttons and typed keys. The developers of the JavaScript language also developed the HTML document object model (DOM). The **DOM** is the list of all the objects and their attributes and methods that a programmer can use to make an HTML document interactive.

Example 11

The following program uses methods and attributes from the DOM to add, change, and remove text fields when the user clicks buttons. The program uses the createElement and appendChild methods to create text fields when a user clicks the Add button. The example uses the getElementsByTagName method to get an array of all the text fields. It uses the size and style attributes to change the size and color of the text fields. Finally, it uses the removeChild method to remove a text field when the user clicks the Remove button. The running program is shown in Figure 11-6.

Figure 11-6: A running JavaScript program that adds, changes, and removes text fields when a user clicks a button.

```
<!DOCTYPE HTML>
<html lang="en-us">
<head>
<meta charset="utf-8">
<title>Changing Text Fields</title>

<script>
/* Adds a text field at the end of the body. */
function addTextField() {
    // Create a unique identifier for the new text field.
    var texts = document.getElementsByTagName('input');
    var id = 'text' + texts.length;

    // Create a text field and set its id.
    var text = document.createElement('input');
    text.type = 'text';
    text.id = id;

    // Create a div and add the text field to the div.
    var div = document.createElement('div');
    div.appendChild(text);

    // Add the div to the document body.
    document.body.appendChild(div);
}
```

```
/* Changes the color of one text field. */
function changeColor() {
    var colors = [
        'black', 'gray', 'brown', 'blue', 'purple', 'red',
        'green', 'chartreuse', 'yellow', 'orange', 'fuchsia', 'white'
    ];

    // Get an array of all text fields.
    var texts = document.getElementsByTagName('input');
    if (texts.length > 0) {

        // Choose a background and a foreground color.
        var index = choose(colors);
        var opposite = colors.length - index - 1;
        var background = colors[index];
        var foreground = colors[opposite];

        // Choose a text field.
        var text = texts[choose(texts)];

        // Change the element's colors.
        text.style.color = foreground;
        text.style.backgroundColor = background;
        text.value = foreground + ' on ' + background;
    }
}


/* Changes the size of all text fields. */
function changeSize() {
    // Get an array of all text fields.
    var texts = document.getElementsByTagName('input');
    if (texts.length > 0) {

        // Get the size of the first element.
        var size = texts[0].size;

        // Increment the size.
        if (++size > 30) {
            size = 5;
        }

        // Change the size of all text fields.
        for (var i = 0;  i < texts.length;  i++) {
            var text = texts[i];
            text.size = size;
        }
    }
}
```

Programming Fundamentals in JavaScript

```
/* Removes a pseudo randomly chosen text field. */
function removeTextField() {
    // Get an array of all text fields.
    var texts = document.getElementsByTagName('input');
    if (texts.length > 0) {

        // Choose a text field.
        var index = choose(texts);
        var text = texts[index];

        // Get the text field's parent.
        var div = text.parentElement;

        // Remove the parent and the text field.
        document.body.removeChild(div);

        // Renumber the id's of the remaining text fields.
        for (var i = index;  i < texts.length;  i++) {
            var id = 'text' + i;
            texts[i].id = id;
        }
    }
}


/* Returns a pseudo random integer in the range [0, list.length). */
function choose(list) {
    var index = Math.floor(Math.random() * list.length);
    return index;
}
</script>
</head>

<body>
<button type="button" onclick="addTextField()">Add</button>
<button type="button" onclick="changeColor()">Color</button>
<button type="button" onclick="changeSize()">Size</button>
<button type="button" onclick="removeTextField()">Remove</button>
</body>
</html>
```

Chapter Summary

- Object oriented programming is a way of viewing the world and designing and implementing software that matches the world.

- An object is anything in the world that has identity, data, behavior, and relationships to other objects.

- A class is both a group of similar objects and a pattern for creating objects.

- The Unified Modeling Language (UML) is a diagramming language that enables a software developer to draw classes and objects.

- JavaScript includes several prototype objects including `Array`, `Boolean`, `Date`, `Number`, `String`, and `RegExp`, that a programmer can use to create new objects.

- To create a JavaScript object use the `new` keyword and the name of the prototype object:
  var *objectName* = new *PrototypeName*();

- To read or write the value of an object's attribute, use the name of the object and the name of the attribute separated by a period:
  objectName.attributeName

- To call a function that is part of an object, use the object's name and the function's name separated by a period:
  objectName.funcName(arg1, arg2, …);

- A programmer can use a JavaScript object as a dictionary to easily and quickly search for values.

- A programmer can use the built-in object `localStorage` to store values after a program finishes.

- A programmer can make HTML pages interactive by using the objects, attributes, and methods in the document object model (DOM).

Review Questions

1. Write JavaScript code to declare and create a `Number` object named `fifty` that holds the value 50.

2. Write JavaScript code to declare and create a `Date` object named `overflow` that holds the date January 19, 2038.

3. Write JavaScript code to display to a user the value of `PI` from the `Math` object.

4. Write JavaScript code to call the `sqrt` function in the `Math` object to compute the square root of 75.

Programming Assignments

1. Write a program that allows a user to enter a date in the format YYYY/MM/DD (a four digit year, a slash, a two digit month, a slash, and a two digit day of the month). Your program should output the name of the day of the week for that date. For example, if the user entered "2016/05/22", your program would output "Sunday". Hint: your program should create a Date object and use the method Date.getDay().

2. Write a program that allows a user to enter two dates in the format YYYY/MM/DD and outputs the difference in days between those two dates. Hint: your program should
   a. create two Date objects
   b. call the Date.getTime() method for both objects which will return the number of milliseconds since January 1, 1970
   c. subtract the millisecond values
   d. divide the difference by 86400000 (1000 * 60 * 60 * 24) to convert from milliseconds to days

3. Mother's Day is celebrated in the United States on the second Sunday of May. Write a program that allows a user to enter a year and then outputs the date that Mother's Day will be celebrated in that year. For example, if the user entered 2018, your program would output "Sunday, May 13, 2018" (without the quotes).

4. Father's Day is celebrated in the United States on the third Sunday of June. Write a program that allows a user to enter a year and then outputs the date that Father's Day will be celebrated in that year. For example, if the user entered 2018, your program would output "Sunday, June 17, 2018" (without the quotes).

Chapter 12. Strings

Within a computer program, the term **string** refers to a string of text or a group of characters strung together. When writing JavaScript code, a good way to visualize a string is as an array of individual characters inside an object with 0 as the index of the first character.

Chapter Outcomes

By the end of this chapter, you will be able to:

- Create strings that include special characters as escape sequences.
- Use the length attribute of a string.
- Access a single character within a string.
- Compare two strings.
- Use the built-in string methods.

Creating a String

To create a string you can use a string literal inside single (') or double (") quotes or the new keyword.

Templates

```
var name = 'any text here';
var name = "any text here";
var name = new String(thing);
```

where *thing* is any valid JavaScript expression to be converted to a string.

Example 1

```
var title = 'Oh Say, What is Truth?';
var other = "Truth Reflects upon Our Senses";
var another = new String('Put Your Shoulder to the Wheel');
```

Example 2

```
var x = 3;
var s = new String(x);
```

String Concatenation

To create a large string of text from smaller strings of text you can use the **string concatenation** operator, which is the plus symbol (+). For example:

Example 3

```
var name = "Samantha";
var message = "Hello, " + name + ". How are you today?";
```

Escape Sequences

Occasionally you will want to include single or double quotes or other special characters in a string literal. You can include a special character by placing a backslash character (\) immediately before it. Within a string literal, a backslash followed by one or more characters is called an **escape sequence**. You can also write escape sequences to include Unicode characters (see unicode.org/charts) in a string literal that you would not be able to type from your keyboard. This includes mathematical symbols and characters from languages other than English.

JavaScript Escape Sequences

Sequence	Description
\b	Backspace
\f	Form feed
\n	New line
\r	Carriage return
\t	Horizontal tab
\v	Vertical tab
\0	Null character
\'	Single quote
\"	Double quote
\\	Backslash
\udddd	The Unicode character specified by the four hexadecimal digits dddd. For example the copyright symbol (©) is \u00a9.

Example 4

```
var quote = "Mr. Churchill declared, \"Never give in!\"";
var greek = 'The first three letters of the Greek alphabet are \u03b1 \u03b2
\u03b3';
```

Within a string literal, the backslash at the end of a line causes the string literal to continue on to the next line.

Example 5

```
    var intersect = 'The mathematical symbol for \
intersection is an upside down U like this: \u2229';
```

String Length

Just like arrays, all strings in JavaScript automatically have an attribute named length, which is the number of characters contained in the string.

Template

```
name.length
```

Example 6

```
var title = 'Carry On';
document.getElementById('output').innerHTML = title.length; // displays 8
```

Accessing a Character

Just like an array, you can use the bracket operators ([and]) to retrieve a single character from a string. Also just like an array, the index of the very first character in a string is 0.

Template

```
var varName = strName[index];
```

Example 7

```
var title = 'Carry On';
var c = title[4];  // the variable c will hold 'y'
```

Because a JavaScript string is an array inside an object, each string has several methods that you can call. The charAt method does the same thing as the bracket operators: retrieve the character at a given location.

Example 8

```
var title = 'Carry On';
var c = title.charAt(4);  // the variable c will hold 'y'
```

Reversing a String

Occasionally you will want to reverse the order of the characters in a string. This is easily done with a loop and string concatenation.

Example 9

```
// Reverses the contents of a string.
function reverse(s) {
    var rev = '';
    for (var i = s.length - 1;  i >= 0;  i--) {
        rev += s.charAt(i);
    }
    return rev;
}
```

Desk Check

s	i	rev
"pool"		

Comparing Strings

To compare strings in JavaScript, you can use the relational operators (<, >, <=, >=, ==, and !=) just as you would for numbers.

Example 9

```
var a = 'always';
var b = 'believe';
var c = 'always';

var output;
if (a < b) {
    output = a + ' is less than ' + b + '. ';
}
else {
    output = a + ' is equal or greater than ' + b + '. ';
}

if (a == c) {
    output += a + ' equals ' + c + '.';
}
else {
    output += a + ' does not equal ' + c + '.';
}

document.getElementById('outputDiv').innerHTML = output;
```

Desk Check

a	b	c	output
"always"	"believe"	"always"	

String Methods

JavaScript includes several useful string methods that you can use to manipulate the contents of strings. Many of these methods are listed in the next table. When calling these methods, a programmer must write the name of the string in front of the method name as shown in this template.

Template

```
stringName.methodName(arg1, arg2, … argN);
```

String Methods

Method	Description
s.charAt(index)	Returns the character at the given index.
s.charCodeAt(index)	Returns a number indicating the Unicode value of the character at the given index.
s.concat(s2, s3, …, sN)	Combines the text of two or more strings and returns a new string.
s.endsWith(toFind, start)	Returns true if the string s ends with the characters of the string toFind.
s.indexOf(toFind, start)	Returns the index within the string s of the first occurrence of the string toFind, or -1 if not found.
s.lastIndexOf(toFind, start)	Returns the index within the string s of the last occurrence of the string toFind, or -1 if not found.
s.replace(toFind, replacement)	Used to find a match between a regular expression and a string, and to replace the matched substring with a new substring.
s.split(sep, limit)	Splits a string into an array of strings by separating the string into substrings.
s.startsWith(toFind, start)	Returns true if the string s starts with the characters of the string toFind.
s.substr(start, length)	Returns the characters of a string starting at the specified index and continuing for the specified number of characters.
s.substring(start, end)	Returns the characters of a string between two indexes into the string.
s.toLowerCase()	Returns a copy of the string s with all characters converted to lower case.
s.toUpperCase()	Returns a copy of the string s with all characters converted to upper case.
s.trim()	Trims whitespace from the beginning and end of the string.

Extracting a Substring

Many computer programs store people's names in this format: *FamilyName, GivenName* (a person's family name followed by a comma and a space followed by the person's given name). When names are stored in this format, a common operation is to extract the family name as done in this function.

Example 11

```
// Extracts a person's family name from his full name.
// This function assumes fullName contains a string in
// this format:  FamilyName, GivenName
function extractFamilyName(fullName) {
    var comma = fullName.indexOf(', ');
    var family = fullName.substring(0, comma);
    return family;
}
```

Desk Check

fullName	comma	family
"Washington, George"		

Counting Characters

Another common operation with strings is to count how many times a specific character occurs in a string. This can be done with a loop and an if statement.

Example 12

```
// Returns the number of times that the
// character stored in c occurs in the string s.
function countOccurrences(s, c) {
    var count = 0;
    for (var i = 0;  i < s.length;  i++) {
        if (s.charAt(i) == c) {
            count++;
        }
    }
    return count;
}
```

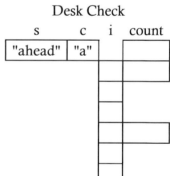

Desk Check

s	c	i	count
"ahead"	"a"		

You may also want to know how many upper case letters are in a string, which can be done very similarly to the previous example.

Example 13

```
// Returns a count of the number of upper case letters in s.
function countUppers(s) {
    var uppers = 'ABCDEFGHIJKLMNOPQRSTUVWXYZ';
    var count = 0;
    for (var i = 0;  i < s.length;  i++) {
        var c = s.charAt(i);
        if (uppers.indexOf(c) != -1) {
            count++;
        }
    }
    return count;
}
```

Desk Check

s	i	c	count
"H. W. Bush"			

Transposing Chords

In music theory, a chord name contains two parts: a note name and an optional suffix. There are twelve note names: A, Bb, B, C, C#, D, Eb, E, F, F#, G, Ab. Within a chord name, the suffix is all the characters after the note name. Some example suffixes are m, 7, m7, maj7, and sus4. If a chord name doesn't contain a suffix, that chord is a major chord.

The next code example is a program that transposes by half steps the chords of a song. The program allows a user to enter multiple chord names and an integer. As shown in Figure 12-1, the user enters in a single text field, the chord names, each separated by a comma and a space. The user enters an integer in its own text field. The integer may be negative or positive and specifies the number of half steps to transpose the chords.

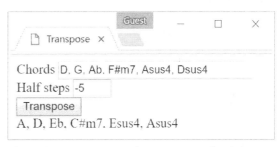

Figure 12-1: A program that transposes chords by half steps.

Notice in the code that the transposeChord function uses an array containing the 12 note names in keyboard order to transpose a chord. The getNote and getSuffix functions use the built-in substr function to separate the parts of a chord name.

Example 14

```
<!DOCTYPE HTML>
<html lang="en-us">
<head>
<meta charset="utf-8">
<meta name="author" content="Rex Barzee">
```

```
<title>Transpose</title>
<script>
/* Input: Chord names and an integer
 * Processing:
 *      A loop that repeats once for each chord
 *          Transpose the chord
 *          Append the transposed chord onto an output string.
 * Output: The transposed chords
 */
function transposeAll() {
        // Get the chord names entered by the user as a string.
        var input = document.getElementById('chords').value;

        // Split the string into an array of chord names.
        var chords = input.split(', ');

        // Get the number of half steps to transpose the chords.
        var halfSteps = parseInt(document.getElementById('halfSteps').value);

        var sep = '';
        var output = '';
        for (var i = 0;  i < chords.length;  ++i) {
                // Retrieve one chord from the array of chords.
                var chord = chords[i];

                // Transpose one chord.
                var transposed = transposeChord(chord, halfSteps);

                // Append the transposed chord to the output.
                output += sep + transposed;
                sep = ', ';
        }

        // Display the transposed chords for the user to see.
        document.getElementById('output').innerHTML = output;
}


/* Parameters:
 *      chord - a string that is a chord name.
 *          Ex: D, Eb, Cm, A7, Fmaj7
 *      halfSteps - an integer that is the number
 *          of half steps to transpose the chord
 * Processing:
 *      Separate the chord name into a note name and a suffix.
 *      Find the index of the original note name.
 *      Transpose the note name by adding the half steps to the index.
 *      Normalize the index so that it is between 0 and 11, inclusive.
 *      Use the index to find the transposed note name.
 *      Combine the transposed note name and suffix into a new chord name.
 * Return: The transposed chord name
 */
```

Programming Fundamentals in JavaScript

```
function transposeChord(chord, halfSteps) {
        // An array that contains all 12 note names in keyboard order.
        var notes = [
                'A', 'Bb', 'B', 'C', 'C#', 'D',
                'Eb', 'E', 'F', 'F#', 'G', 'Ab'
        ];

        // Separate the note name and suffix from the chord name.
        var note = getNote(chord);
        var suffix = getSuffix(chord);

        // Find where the note name is stored in the array of all 12 note names.
        var index = notes.indexOf(note);

        // Transpose the original note by adding the half steps.
        index += halfSteps;

        // If the half steps value is negative and the
        // transposed index is less than 0, then repeatedly
        // add 12 to the index until it is non-negative.
        while (index < 0) {
                index += notes.length;
        }

        // If the half steps value is positive and the
        // transposed index is 12 or greater, then repeatedly
        // subtract 12 from the index until it is less than 12.
        while (index >= notes.length) {
                index -= notes.length;
        }

        // Build the transposed chord name by concatenating
        // the transposed note name to the chord suffix.
        var transposed = notes[index] + suffix;

        return transposed;
}

/* Parameter: chord - a string that is a chord name.
 *      Ex: D, Eb, Cm, A7, Fmaj7
 * Processing: Extract a substring from the chord name.
 * Return: the note name from the chord.
 *      Ex: D, Eb, C, A, F
 */
function getNote(chord) {
        var len = 1;
        if (chord.length > 1 && (chord[1] == 'b' || chord[1] == '#')) {
                len = 2;
        }
        var note = chord.substr(0, len);
        return note;
}
```

```
/* Parameter: chord - a string that is a chord name.
 *      Ex: D, Eb, Cm, A7, Fmaj7
 * Processing:
 *      Get the note name from the chord name.
 *      Extract a substring from the chord name.
 * Return: the suffix from the chord. Ex: m, 7, maj7
 */
function getSuffix(chord) {
        var note = getNote(chord);
        var suffix = chord.substr(note.length);
        return suffix;
}
</script>
</head>

<body>
Chords <input type="text" id="chords" size="30"><br>
Half steps <input type="text" id="halfSteps" size="2"><br>
<button type="button" onclick="transposeAll()">Transpose</button>
<div id="output"></div>
</body>
</html>
```

Chapter Summary

- To create a string surround text with single or double quotes.
- To include special characters, such as single quote ('), double quote ("), or new line, in a string use an escape sequence: \' \" \n etc.
- To read or write a single character within a string, use the bracket operators [and] like an array: *stringName*[*index*];
- To compare to strings, use the comparison operators: ==, !=, <, <=, >, and >=
- JavaScript contains many useful built-in string methods.

Review Questions

1. Write JavaScript code to declare a string named address and assign the text "123 W Main" to it.

2. What character is at index 4 in the string literal in the previous question?

3. Write JavaScript code to retrieve the character at index 4 from the variable address and to store that character in a variable named c.

4. Write JavaScript code to convert all the characters in a string named s to lower case and assign the lower case string to a variable named t.

Programming Assignments

1. Write a function named `extractGivenName` with one parameter named `fullName`. The parameter `fullName` will always contain a person's family and given names in that order separated by a comma and a single space, for example "Reagan, Ronald" (without the quotation marks). The function should extract and return the person's given name, for example "Ronald" (without the quotation marks).

2. Write a function named `prefix` that returns the common prefix of two strings. For example, the common prefix of "disable" and "distasteful" is "dis". This function takes two parameters and returns the common prefix.

3. Write a function named `suffix` that returns the common suffix of two strings. For example, the common suffix of "swimming" and "walking" is "ing". This function takes two parameters and returns the common suffix.

4. Write a function named `switchCase` that receives a parameter named `s`. This function must return a new string that contains the same characters as `s` but with the case of every character switched. For example, if `switchCase` were called like this: `switchCase("Catch 22")`; it would return `"cATCH 22"` (without the quotes).

5. Write a function named `titleCase` with one parameter named `s`. This function returns a copy of `s` but with the first letter of each word capitalized.

Appendix A. Operator Precedence

Operator precedence determines the order in which the computer evaluates operators. Operators with higher precedence are evaluated first. For example, 7 + 3 * 2 is 13 because multiplication has a higher precedence than addition, so the computer performs the multiplication before the addition.

Associativity

Operator associativity determines the order in which the computer evaluates operators of the same precedence. There are two categories of associativity, left to right and right to left. Consider the expression: a OP1 b OP2 c

Left to Right Associativity

If OP_1 and OP_2 have the same precedence and left associativity (left to right) then the computer will evaluate the expression as: (a OP_1 b) OP_2 c
For example, the computer evaluates 3 − 5 + 4 as (3 − 5) + 4 which is 2.

Right to Left Associativity

If OP_1 and OP_2 have the same precedence and right associativity (right to left) then the computer will evaluate the expression as : a OP_1 (b OP_2 c)
For example, the computer evaluates a = b = 5 as a = (b = 5) by first storing 5 in b, then storing the value of b in a.

Precedence

Listed from highest precedence (evaluated first) to lowest precedence

Operator(s)	Name(s)	Associativity
( )	parentheses	n/a
. [ ]	member	left to right
++ --	increment, decrement	n/a
+ - ! ~	unary plus, negation, logical not, bitwise not	right to left
* / %	multiplication, division, modulus	left to right
+ -	addition, subtraction	left to right
<< >> >>>	bitwise shift	left to right
< > <= >=	relational	left to right
== !=	equality	left to right
&	bitwise and	left to right
^	bitwise exclusive or (xor)	left to right
|	bitwise or	left to right
&&	logical and	left to right
||	logical or	left to right
? :	conditional	right to left
= += -= *= /= %= <<= >>= >>>= &= ^= |=	assignment operators	right to left
,	comma	left to right

Appendix B. Robust Code

There is an old computer programming joke that goes like this. A consultant went to a large company to teach the software engineers in the company. At the beginning of the class she said to the students, "If you got on an airplane and realized that your team had written the software that runs the airplane, how many of you would be afraid for your life and get off the plane?" Every student except one put his hand up. The consultant looked at the one student who didn't raise his hand and asked, "What does your team do differently so that you wouldn't be afraid to ride on the airplane?"

The student answered, "Ha! If my team had written the software, the plane would never even get off the ground. I'd be perfectly safe."

Below are some programming practices that if you follow will make your software more robust (fewer errors) and help you rest easy on a working airplane for which you and your team wrote the software.

1. Turn on compiler warnings and never ignore them.
2. Follow generally accepted coding standards and conventions, including naming conventions.
3. Write and use assertions. Test primarily with assertions turned on.
4. Write and execute unit tests and don't ignore test failures.
5. Whenever possible, write simple, straight forward code. For example, when writing in JavaScript, Java, C++, and C do not use the left shift operator (<<) to multiply by a power of two. Instead, use multiplication (*) and rely on the compiler to generate fast code.
6. Write each function to perform one and only one task.
7. Minimize the number of execution paths through your code. For example, an if statement creates two separate paths through code: one path when the if statement comparison is true and another path when the comparison is false. (See the section Finding a Range in chapter 10 of this book for an example of how to do this.)
8. Write each function with only one exit point (return statement).
9. Consider writing a tricky algorithm twice, once with a straight forward, slow solution and once with a sophisticated, fast solution. In the debugging version of your program, use the slow solution to verify the results of the fast solution.
10. When writing in a language that has exceptions, never return error codes from a function. Instead, throw exceptions to indicate an error.

Appendix C. Answers to Selected Desk Checks

Chapter 5. Variables and Arithmetic

5.6 Swap

a	b	swap
~~8~~	~~−3~~	8
−3	8	

5.10 fahrToCels

text	f	f − 32	5 / 9	c
"25"	25	−7	0.56	−3.92

5.20 Pre Increment

x	y
~~3~~	13
4	

5.21 Post Increment

x	y
~~3~~	11
4	

5.23 Cylinder Volume

r	h	v
2.7	5	114.51

5.24 Round

x1	y1	x2	y2	dx	dy	dist	digits	multiplier
7	−2	4	6	3	8	~~8.5440037~~	2	100
						8.54		

Chapter 6. Selection

6.5 isEven

text	value	value % 2	message
"8"	8	0	"8 is an even integer"

6.9 Quadratic

a	b	c	discr	sq	root1	root2
1	−4	3	4	2	3	1

6.12 ticketPrice

age	gamesAttended	price
38	6	10.0

Chapter 7. Logic

7.2 Group

age	group
14	"Mia Maid"

7.3 Group

age	group
15	"Venture"

7.4 Autopia

driver	passenger	message
48	56	"Enjoy the ride!"

Chapter 8. Repetition

8.1 While

i
~~1~~
~~2~~
3

8.2 For

i
~~1~~
~~2~~
3

8.9

i
~~0~~
~~1~~
~~2~~
3

8.10

i
~~0~~
~~4~~
~~8~~
12

8.10 Compound Interest

annualRate	monthlyRate	numMonths	month	interest	balance
0.06	0.005	3			~~100~~
			~~1~~	0.5	
				0.5	~~100.5~~
			~~2~~	0.5025	
				0.5	~~101~~
			~~3~~	0.505	
				0.51	101.51
			4		

8.11 Sum

i	n	sum
		~~0~~
~~0~~	~~17~~	~~17~~
~~1~~	~~−3~~	~~14~~
~~2~~	~~6~~	20
3	0	

8.12 isPrime

candidate	divisor	remainder	factorCount	output
8			~~0~~	"8 is not prime"
	~~1~~	~~0~~	~~1~~	
	~~2~~	~~0~~	~~2~~	
	~~3~~	~~2~~		
	~~4~~	~~0~~	~~3~~	
	~~5~~	~~3~~		
	~~6~~	~~2~~		
	~~7~~	~~1~~		
	~~8~~	0	4	
	9			

8.13 isPrime

candidate	limit	prime	divisor	remainder	output
8	2.83	~~true~~	2	0	"8 is not prime"
		false			

8.14 Repetitive String

i	output
	~~"0"~~
~~2~~	~~"0, 2"~~
~~4~~	~~"0, 2, 4"~~
~~6~~	~~"0, 2, 4, 6"~~
~~8~~	~~"0, 2, 4, 6, 8"~~
~~10~~	"0, 2, 4, 6, 8, 10"
12	

Chapter 9. Functions

9.10 Pseudo Random Integer

min	max	value returned from Math.random	r
5	11	0.483	7

9.12 isEven

number	result
8	"8 is even: true"

value	value % 2	return
8	0	true

9.14 Pyramid Surface Area

pa
129.0

base	height	edge	triArea	pyramidArea
8	7	9	32.25	129.0

a	b	c	s	(s − a)	(s − b)	(s − c)	area
8	9	9	13	5	4	4	32.25

9.16 GCD

x	y	divisor
−24	472	8

r	a	b	swap	return value
	-24	472	24	8
	24	472		
	472	24		
16	24	16		
8	16	8		
0	8	0		

Chapter 10. Arrays

10.10 Fill

list

8.3	8.3	8.3	8.3
[0]	[1]	[2]	[3]

x	i
8.3	~~0~~
	~~1~~
	~~2~~
	~~3~~
	4

10.12 Reverse Ramp

list

4	3	2	1	0
[0]	[1]	[2]	[3]	[4]

high	i
4	~~0~~
	~~1~~
	~~2~~
	~~3~~
	~~4~~
	5

10.13 Reverse

list

~~3.4~~	~~-2~~	~~5~~	~~7~~	~~12~~
12	7	5	-2	3.4
[0]	[1]	[2]	[3]	[4]

left	right	swap
~~0~~	~~4~~	~~3.4~~
~~1~~	~~3~~	-2
2	2	

10.14 Sum

list				
3.4	-2	5	7	12
[0]	[1]	[2]	[3]	[4]

i	s	return
	~~0~~	25.4
~~0~~	~~3.4~~	
~~1~~	~~1.4~~	
~~2~~	~~6.4~~	
~~3~~	~~13.4~~	
~~4~~	25.4	
5		

10.16 Parallel Arrays

studentIDs

"07-153-4276"	"34-513-3186"	"26-430-0198"
[0]	[1]	[2]

studentNames

"Felix"	"Jonathan"	"Grace"
[0]	[1]	[3]

studID	index	name
"34-513-3186"	1	"Jonathan"

key	i	index
"34-513-3186"	~~0~~	~~-1~~
	1	1

10.18 Find a Range

purchase	rate	discount	return
$708.00	0.025	17.7	690.3

10.19 Find a Range

limits

300	600	1000
[0]	[1]	[2]

rates

0	0.02	0.025	0.03
[0]	[1]	[2]	[3]

purchase	i	rate	discount	return
$708.00	~~0~~	0.025	17.7	690.3
	~~1~~			
	2			

10.21 Binary Search

list

−2.1	−1	3.9	6.2	7.1	9.7	10	12	13.1	15.6	18	19	20.1	24.5
[0]	[1]	[2]	[3]	[4]	[5]	[6]	[7]	[8]	[9]	[10]	[11]	[12]	[13]

key	left	right	mid	cmp	return
15.6	~~0~~	~~13~~	~~6~~	~~5.6~~	9
	~~7~~		~~10~~	~~−2.4~~	
		9	~~8~~	~~2.5~~	
	9		9	0	

Chapter 12. Strings

12.9 Reverse String

s	i	rev
"pool"		~~""~~
	~~3~~	~~"l"~~
	~~2~~	~~"lo"~~
	~~1~~	~~"loo"~~
	~~0~~	"loop"
	−1	

12.10 Compare Strings

a	b	c	output
"always"	"believe"	"always"	~~"always is less than believe. "~~
			"always is less than believe. always equals always."

12.11 Extract Family Name

fullName	comma	family
"Washington, George"	11	"Washington"

12.13 Count Uppers

s	i	c	count
"H. W. Bush"			~~0~~
	~~0~~	~~"H"~~	~~1~~
	~~1~~	~~"."~~	
	~~2~~	~~" "~~	
	~~3~~	~~"W"~~	~~2~~
	~~4~~	~~"."~~	
	~~5~~	~~" "~~	
	~~6~~	~~"B"~~	3
	~~7~~	~~"u"~~	
	~~8~~	~~"s"~~	
	~~9~~	"h"	
	10		

Appendix D.
Answers to Selected Review Questions

Chapter 1. Computer Hardware

1. Which of the following computer components primarily stores data? (Mark all that apply.)
    a. power supply
    b. keyboard
    c. motherboard
    d. bus
    e. central processing unit (CPU)
    f. ✓ cache
    g. ✓ main memory
    h. ✓ hard drive
    i. ✓ DVD drive
    j. ✓ thumb drive
    k. monitor

3. Computer memory that is volatile must have electricity in order to store data. When electricity is turned off, volatile memory loses its data. Non-volatile memory stores data after electricity is turned off. Which of the following computer memory devices are volatile? (Mark all that apply.)
    a. ✓ cache
    b. ✓ main memory
    c. flash memory
    d. hard drive
    e. DVD

5. Assume the average movie uses 3 gigabytes of space on a hard drive. Which of these is the smallest size that can store 200 average size movies?
    a. 500 megabytes
    b. 500 gigabytes
    c. ✓ 1 terabyte
    d. 1 petabyte

7. Which character coding system includes English letters? (Mark all that apply.)
    a. ✓ ASCII
    b. ✓ Unicode

Chapter 2. Algorithms and Computer Programs

1. Your company needs a program to compute the amount to charge customers for mowing their lawns for an entire season. An employee will type in the total area of the customer's lawn in square feet. Your company charges 1 cent per square foot to mow a lawn one time and will mow each lawn once a week for 15 weeks. Match each of the following parts of this problem to its correct location in a defining table.

    2. multiply by 15
    3. season cost
    1. area of lawn   1. Input
    2. multiply by 0.01   2. Processing
                         3. Output

2. Your company needs a program to compute the amount to charge customers for mowing their lawns for an entire season. An employee will type in the total area of the customer's lawn in square feet. Your company charges 1 cent per square foot to mow a lawn one time and will mow each lawn once a week for 15 weeks. Number each of these steps to solve the problem in the correct order from first (1) to last (3).

    2. Multiply the area of the lawn by 0.01 and then by 15 to get the season cost.
    3. Display the season cost for the user to see.
    1. Get the total area of the lawn from the user.

5. Which of the following are control structures? (Mark all that apply.)
    a. input
    b. ✓ try, catch, and throw
    c. computation
    d. ✓ selection
    e. ✓ sequence
    f. output
    g. ✓ repetition
    h. storage

Chapter 3. HTML Basics

2. Write the HTML 5 document type declaration as it should appear at the top of all HTML 5 documents. Include the surrounding less than (<) and greater than (>) symbols in your answer.

    ```
    <!DOCTYPE HTML>
    ```

4. What are the two main sections that every HTML 5 document must have?

    The head and the body

6. What is the tag to begin the largest type of heading? Include the surrounding less than (<) and greater than (>) symbols in your answer.

    ```
    <h1>
    ```

8. Write the HTML tag and its attributes for creating a text field. Include the surrounding less than (<) and greater than (>) symbols in your answer.

```
<input type="text">
```

10. What is the attribute that a programmer can use to uniquely identify each element within an HTML document?

```
id
```

12. What is the tag that ends an HTML document? Include the surrounding less than (<) and greater than (>) symbols in your answer.

```
</html>
```

Chapter 4. JavaScript Basics

1. What is the HTML tag that begins a section of JavaScript code? Include the surrounding less than (<) and greater than (>) symbols in your answer.

```
<script>
```

3. What does the document.getElementById function do?
   a. display a message in a pop-up window and get input from a user
   b. ✓ find an element within an HTML document
   c. convert a number to text
   d. convert text to a number

5. Write the HTML tag that makes a text field that can be used by this JavaScript statement:

```
var addr = document.getElementById('address').value;
```

   Include the surrounding less than (<) and greater than (>) symbols and necessary attributes in your answer.

```
<input type="text" id="address">
```

7. What is the attribute of a button that contains JavaScript code that will be executed when a user clicks on that button?

```
onclick
```

Chapter 5. Variables and Arithmetic

2. Declare a variable named inventor and assign the text "Franklin" to it.

```
var inventor = "Franklin";
```

4. What does the `parseFloat` function do?
   a. convert a number to text
   b. ✓ convert text to a number
   c. display a message in a pop-up window and get input from a user
   d. use an ID to find an element in a document

6. After a computer executes the following JavaScript code, variable *b* will be of what data type? Hint: pay attention to the double quotes.
   ```
   var b = "true";
   ```

   string

8. After a computer executes the following JavaScript code, variable *e* will be of what data type and hold what value?
   ```
   var c = 15;
   var d = -2.17;
   var e = c + d;
   ```

   number

10. After a computer executes the following JavaScript code, variable *k* will be of what data type?
    ```
    var i = document.getElementById('number1').value;
    var j = document.getElementById('number2').value;
    var k = i + j;
    ```

    string because user input is always text. If we want user input to be a number, we must use `parseInt` or `parseFloat`. Notice that they are missing in the above code, so *i* and *j* will be strings and *k* will also be a string because it is the result of string concatenation.

12. After a computer executes the following JavaScript code, variable *r* will be of what data type and hold what value?
    ```
    var c = 15;
    var r = "You found " + c + " coins.";
    ```

    string

14. The semi-perimeter, *s*, of a triangle with side lengths *a*, *b*, and *c* is given by the formula
    $$s = \frac{a + b + c}{2}$$

    Translate this formula into JavaScript. Assume that the variables *a*, *b*, and *c* already exist and each holds a value. When writing your answer, be sure to declare *s* and use the variable names given in the equation above.

```
var s = (a + b + c) / 2;
```

16. Rewrite the JavaScript statement:
    ```
    z += x - 3 * y;
    ```
    so that it doesn't use the += operator.

    ```
    z = z + (x - 3 * y);
    ```

Chapter 6. Selection

1. Write an if statement to determine if the value in the variable *age* is greater than 12.

    ```
    if (age > 12) {
    ```

3. Write an if statement that displays "go south" if the value in the variable *temperature* is less than 32, and displays "enjoy" otherwise.

    ```
    if (temperature < 32) {
        alert('go south');
    }
    else {
        alert('enjoy');
    }
    ```

5. The following if statement contains an error. Rewrite it so that it is correct. Assume the variable age already exists and holds a valid number.
    ```
        if age < 8 {
    ```

    ```
    if (age < 8) {
    ```

7. The following if statement contains an error. Rewrite it so that it is correct. Assume the variable *age* already exists and holds a valid number.
    ```
        if (age =< 55) {
    ```

    ```
    if (age <= 55) {
    ```

9. Given the following JavaScript code, what will the computer output for the user to see?
    ```
        var x = 1, y = 7;
        var message = "Welcome";
        if (x < 2) {
            if (y > 10) {
                message = "Hello";
            }
            else {
                message = "Goodbye";
            }
        }
        alert(message);
    ```

Goodbye

Chapter 7. Logic

2. The following `if` statement contains a logic error, not a syntax error. Rewrite it so that it is correct. Assume the variable *age* already exists and holds a valid number.
    ```
    if (18 < age || age < 30) {
    ```

    ```
    if (18 < age && age < 30) {
    ```

4. After the following code executes, what value will the variable *result* hold?
    ```
    var x = 2, y = 6, z = 5;
    var result = (x < 3 && (y < 7 ^ z != 3))
    ```

    false

6. Use the advanced search at google to find on the internet a recipe for pizza that doesn't include tomato sauce. Besides the dough, what ingredients does the recipe use? What was the complete search criteria that you used?

    pizza recipe -"tomato sauce"
    or
    pizza recipe no tomato sauce

8. Use a truth table to prove that Not (a And b) ⇔ Not a Or Not b

1	*2*	*4*	*3*		*5*	*7*	*6*
a	**b**	**!**	**(a && b)**	⇔	**!a**	**||**	**!b**
False	False	True	False		True	True	True
False	True	True	False		True	True	False
True	False	True	False		False	True	True
True	True	False	True		False	False	False

Notice that the values in columns *4* and *7* are the same,
thus Not (a And b) ⇔ Not a Or Not b

10. Write a truth table for this Boolean expression: (a Or b) And Not (a Xor b)

1	*2*	*3*	*5*	*7*	*6*
a	**b**	**(a || b)**	**&&**	**!**	**(a ^ b)**
False	False	False	False	True	False
False	True	True	False	False	True
True	False	True	False	False	True
True	True	True	True	True	False

Does the result seem familiar? Is it possible to rewrite this boolean expression more simply and get the same result? What is the simplified expression?
Yes, a And b

	1	2	3
	a	b	(a && b)
	False	False	False
	False	True	False
	Truc	Falsc	Falsc
	True	True	True

Chapter 8. Repetition

1. Given the following JavaScript code, how many times will the computer display the word "Flowers"?

```
for (var i = 3;  i < 7;  i++) {
    alert("Flowers");
}
```

four times

3. Given the following JavaScript code, how many times will the computer display the word "Goodbye"?

```
for (var i = 0;  i > 3;  i++) {
    alert("Goodbye");
}
```

zero times

5. Write a while loop to count from 1 to 10.

```
var i = 1;
while (i < 10) {
    i++;
}
```

7. Write a loop to count by threes from zero to nine. After the loop is finished, your counting variable should hold the value 9.

```
for (var i = 0;  i < 9;  i += 3) {
```

9. Write a loop to count forwards by twos from the value in the variable first to the value in the variable last. Assume the variables first and last already exist and hold values.

```
for (var i = first;  i < last;  i += 2) {
```

11. Desk check the following code and then write a sentence describing what the code does.

```javascript
function func1() {
    var c = "";
 var a = parseInt(document.getElementById('integerBox').value);
    var b = 100;
        while (b >= 0) {
 c += b + "<br>";
        b -= a;
            }
    document.getElementById('outputDiv').innerHTML = c;
}
```

Desk Check

a	b	c
20		""
	~~100~~	~~"100 "~~
	~~80~~	~~"100 80 "~~
	~~60~~	~~"100 80 60 "~~
	~~40~~	~~"100 80 60 40 "~~
	~~20~~	~~"100 80 60 40 20 "~~
	~~0~~	"100 80 60 40 20 0 "
	−25	

13. Desk check the following code and then write a sentence describing what the code does.

```javascript
function func4() {
    var d = "Please enter an integer.";
 var b = 38;
    var c;
  do {
        c = parseInt(prompt(d));
      if (c < b) {
      d = "Too low. Please enter another integer.";
            }
      else if (c > b) {
 d = "Too high. Please enter another integer.";
}
      } while (c != b);
  d = c + " is correct!";

  alert(d);
}
```

Desk Check

b	c	d
38		~~"Please enter an integer."~~
	~~25~~	~~"Too low. Please enter another integer."~~
	~~60~~	~~"Too high. Please enter another integer."~~
	38	"38 is correct!"

Chapter 9. Functions

2. What is the JavaScript keyword that begins a function header?

```
function
```

4. Write the header for a function named coneVolume, which takes as parameters a radius and a height.

```
function coneVolume(radius, height) {
```

6. Within a function call, for example:
```
var g = gcd(142, y);
```
the text that appears within parentheses are called what?

parameters

8. Assume that a function with this header:
```
function addOrder(name, amount)
```
already exists. Write a single line of JavaScript code to call that function.

```
addOrder("Serah", 17.25);
```

10. Within a function, what does the keyword return do? (Mark all that apply)
    a. ✓ cause the computer to stop executing the current function
    b. ✓ return a value to the call point
    c. display a value for a user to see
    d. ✓ cause the computer to resume executing code after the call point

Chapter 10. Arrays

1. Given the following JavaScript statement, what is the index of the last element in the array named stuff?
```
var stuff = [ 13, -1.8, 20, 6.3 ];
```

3

3. Given the following array what is the value of s[3] - s[1]?
```
var s = [ 4, -1, 0, 5, 9, 1, 2, 4 ];
```

6

5. Write JavaScript code to call the fill function as given in example 10 of this chapter and pass the array that you created in the previous review question to the fill function.

```
fill(data, 0);
```

7. Write code to output (display to the user) the value stored at index 1 in the samples array.

```
document.getElementById('output').innerHTML = samples[1];
```

Chapter 11. Objects

2. Write JavaScript code to declare and create a Date object named overflow that holds the date January 19, 2038.

```
var overflow = new Date("2038/01/19");
or
var overflow = new Date(2038, 0, 19);
```

4. Write JavaScript code to call the sqrt function in the Math object to compute the square root of 75.

```
var rt = Math.sqrt(75);
```

Chapter 12. Strings

1. Write JavaScript code to declare a string named address and assign the text "123 W Main" to it.

```
var address = "123 W Main";
```

3. Write JavaScript code to retrieve the character at index 4 from the variable address and to store that character in a variable named c.

```
var c = address[4];
```

Index

-- (decrement), 44
− (negation), 39
' (single quote), 27, 193
− (subtraction), 39
! (logical not), 81
!= (not equal), 59
" (double quotes), 27, 193
% (modulus), 39
&& (logical and), 81
( ) (parentheses), 40
* (multiplication), 39
/ (division), 39
/* (multi-line JavaScript comment), 26
// (single line JavaScript comment), 26
[ ]. *See* array index
\ (backslash). *See* escape sequence
^ (exclusive or), 81
^ (logical exclusive or), 87
|| (logical inclusive or), 81
+ (addition), 39
+ (string concatenation). See string
    concatenation
++ (increment), 44
< (less than), 59
<!-- (HTML comment), 15
<= (less than or equal), 59
= (assignment), 39
== (equal to), 59
> (greater than), 59
>= (greater than or equal), 59
aggregation, 178
alert, 27, 28
algorithm, 10
And. *See* &&
array, 147
    element, 147
    index, 147, 149
    length, 149
    subscript. See array index
array methods, 162
Array object, 182
ASCII, 6
association, 179

attribute, 177, 183
bit, 4
boolean, 36, 59
break, 111
byte, 4
case, 66
class, 177
composition, 178
concatenation. See string concatenation
control structure, 12
Date object, 182, 183
De Morgan's laws, 89, 90
defining table, 9
dependency, 179
desk check, ix
dictionary, 184
do while, 104, 106
document object model, 187
else, 61, 64
escape sequence, 194
exclusive or. *See* ^
flow of execution, 12
for, 105, 106
for each, 106
function, 36, 123
    argument, 123, 125, 126
    call point, 126, 138
    header, 123
    parameter, 124, 126, 138
    return, 124, 126, 137
    signature. See function header
gigabyte, 5
gigahertz, 5
Heron's formula, 131
hertz, 5
if, 60
if else, 61
inclusive or. *See* ||
index. *See* array index
inheritance, 178
innerHTML, 29
integer division, 42
kilobyte, 4

local storage, 185
Math object, 47, 182
megabyte, 5
megahertz, 5
method, 123, 177, 184
module, 123, 138
multiplicity, 179
new, 148, 182, 193
new line character, 194
nibble, 4
non-volatile, 4
Not. *See* !
number, 36
object, 36, 177
onclick, 26
Or. *See* ||
parseFloat, 40
parseInt, 41
precedence, 40
prompt, 28
Roman numerals, 80, 176
Rook, 176
scope, 127

global, 127
local, 127
statement, 11, 27
string, 27, 36, 193
concatenation, 27, 193, 196
length, 195
String object, 182, 197
switch, 66
tab character, 194
truth table, 92
undefined, 37
Unicode, 6, 194
Unified Modeling Language, 178
var, 27, 35
variable, 35
data type, 36
declare, 35
name, 35
void tag, 18
volatile, 3
while, 104
Xor. *See* ^

About the Author

Rex A. Barzee is a professor of Computer Information Technology at Brigham Young University – Idaho. He is an inventor of two United States patents and the author of numerous books. He earned a bachelor's and master's degree in Computer Science from Brigham Young University. Before becoming a professor, he worked in industry for eight years as a software engineer for Southwest Research Institute, Hewlett-Packard Company, Voyant Technologies, and the Utah State University Space Dynamics Laboratory. He worked on a variety of projects including the HP-UX kernel, the HP-UX standard C library, HP-UX OpenGL 3D Graphics Library, full text indexing, image processing, and VoiceXML applications. You can see his full profile at LinkedIn.

Other Books by the Author

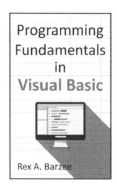

$a = 2$
$b = -3$
$c = 14$
$d = 5 ;$

$6 + 14 / 2 \, 9. \, 5 + (-3)$

$20 / 1 + (-3)$

$6 + (c / a) 9. \quad d + b$

$6 + 14 / 2 \, 9. \, 5 + b3$

$6 + 7 \, 7. 5 - 3$

$6 + 2 - 3$

$8 - 3 \; \textcircled{5} \; ?$

18407590R00135

Made in the USA
San Bernardino, CA
20 December 2018